# Landscape Plans

Created and designed by
the editorial staff of
ORTHO BOOKS

Project Editor
**Barbara Feller-Roth**

Writer
**Ron Lutsko, Jr.**

Illustrator
**Robyn Sherrill Menigoz**

Photographers
**Saxon Holt**
**Michael Lewis**

Photo Editor
**Monica Suder**

Designer
**Gary Hespenheide**

# Ortho Books

**Publisher**
Robert J. Dolezal

**Editorial Director**
Christine Robertson

**Production Director**
Ernie S. Tasaki

**Managing Editors**
Michael D. Smith
Sally W. Smith

**System Manager**
Katherine Parker

**National Sales Manager**
Charles H. Aydelotte

**Marketing Specialist**
Dennis M. Castle

**Operations Assistant**
Georgiann Wright

**Distribution Specialist**
Barbara F. Steadham

**Administrative Assistant**
Francine Lorentz-Olson

**Senior Technical Analyst**
J. A. Crozier, Jr., Ph.D.

Address all inquiries to:
Ortho Books
Box 5006
San Ramon, CA 94583-0906

Copyright © 1989
Monsanto Company
All rights reserved under international and Pan-American copyright conventions.

| 11 | 12 | 13 | 14 | 15 | 16 | 17 |
|----|----|----|----|----|----|----|
| 96 | 97 | 98 | 99 | 00 | 01 | 02 |

ISBN 0-89721-196-0
Library of Congress Catalog Card Number 88-63843

## THE SOLARIS GROUP
2527 Camino Ramon
San Ramon, CA 94583-0906

# Acknowledgments

**Copy Chief**
Melinda E. Levine

**Copyeditor**
Hazel White

**Layout Editor**
Linda M. Bouchard

**Systems Coordinator**
Laurie A. Steele

**Editorial Coordinator**
Cass Dempsey

**Proofreader**
Daniel Ashby

**Indexer**
Shirley J. Manley

**Editorial Assistants**
Nicole Barrett
Deborah N. Bruner
Karen K. Johnson
Tamara Mallory

**Art Director**
Craig Bergquist

**Production by**
Studio 165

**Text separations by**
Palace Press, Singapore

**Cover separations by**
Color Tech Corporation, U.S.A.

**Lithographed in the USA by**
Banta Book Group

**Technical Advisor**
Drew Oman, MLA

**Consultant**
Stephen Drown, Ohio State University

**Contributors**
Stephen Drown, Ohio State University
Robert G. Mower, Cornell University
William Slack, University of Georgia

**Location Scout and Site Researcher**
John Boring

**Photographers**
Names of photographers are followed by the page numbers on which their work appears. R = right, C = center, L = left, T = top, B = bottom.

Josephine Coatsworth/Ortho Slide Library: 19
Saxon Holt: Front cover, title page, 4, 7, 8, 10, 11, 12, 13T, 14B, 16B, 17, 20, 23, 24, 26, 28, 30, 34, 36, 41, 42, 43, 46, 47, 48, 49, 50, 56, 57, 58, 59, 61T, 63, 66, 67, 68, 70, 74, 81, 82, 86, 91, 94, 95, 97T, 98T, 101, 104, 105B, 106, back cover
Michael Landis/Ortho Slide Library: 60
Michael Lewis: 13B, 15, 32, 38, 40, 52, 64, 69, 76, 78, 80, 84
Ron Lutsko, Jr.: 90, 92, 97B, 98B, 99, 102, 103, 105T, 107
Susan A. Roth: 14T, 16T, 44, 61B, 72
Wolf von dem Bussche/Ortho Slide Library: 55

**Landscape Designers and Architects and Site Credits: See page 112**

**Special Thanks To**
Hank Chapot, Mitsuko and Andrew Collver, Louis Edmonds, Rachel Hagner, Grace Hall, Tami Heinle, Marcia Heron, Jim and Christy Jordan, Bill McGowan, Jane McKay, Betty Munier, Marion Panaretos, The Helen Crocker Russell Library, Tom Sholseth DVM, Nancy Sullivan, Dick Turner

**Front Cover**
A well thought-out landscape plan can result in a gracious garden that complements the architecture of your house.

**Title Page**
The rich color of high summer is displayed in this perennial border.

**Back Cover**

**Upper Left:** Carefully controlled curves and contrasting textures entice the viewer into this garden.

**Upper Right:** Brick paving framed by planter boxes brimming with flowering ornamentals transforms this driveway into a handsome entry.

**Lower Left:** Water sheets seamlessly over the edge of this lap pool, which takes dramatic advantage of its sloping site.

**Lower Right:** Tall clipped hedges and crisp-looking white furniture lend a serene feeling to this garden room.

## INTRODUCTION TO PLANNING YOUR LANDSCAPE

Create your own landscape plan by listing your family's landscape needs and by understanding a few basic design principles. This chapter will help you turn your needs into a landscape that is custom designed for your family.

*5*

## ELEMENTS IN THE HOME LANDSCAPE

Let your garden design be inspired by these landscape plans. The discussion of each plan will help you understand what makes it work and how its concepts can be adapted to your site, the architectural style of your house, and your life-style.

*21*

## LANDSCAPE PLANT GUIDE

The best landscape plants for all climate zones are listed in this guide. Choose the plants that thrive in your area. Plants are keyed to the landscape plans in the preceding chapter.

*87*

# Landscape Plans

# Introduction to Planning Your Landscape

*Create your own landscape plan by listing your family's landscape needs and by understanding a few basic design principles. This chapter will help you turn your needs into a landscape that is custom designed for your family.*

The private residential garden can be a place to provoke thought and seek inspiration, a refuge to rest in, an area to play in, a place simply to look at. It can take on many forms, provide varying sensory experiences, and accommodate many types of activities. It can be as simple or as complex as you wish to make it.

To someone designing a private garden, this wide range of uses may seem intimidating. Actually, the private garden is the simplest landscape to create, for the only people it needs to satisfy are the people living in it.

Begin to create your landscape by thinking about how you would like to use the garden, how you want it to look, and why you want it to look that way. It need not be a complicated process; some background information, a well-thought-out set of goals, and an organized approach can bring pleasing results that may even exceed your expectations. Simply going to the local garden center and purchasing some bushes to green up the front will most likely do only that. With thought and planning, you can have a landscape that will reward you with great satisfaction throughout the seasons and for the years to come.

*The gracious proportions of this private entry garden frame and complement the traditional home. The quiet richness of brick walls and paving, clipped hedges, and turf lawn ties the house, with its simple detailing and somber colors, to the perennial borders, with their mix of textures and vibrant colors.*

## UNDERSTANDING THE LANDSCAPE

Observation is an excellent learning tool. It is even more effective if you thoroughly understand what you see. This book will deepen your understanding of the gardens that inspire you and the design concepts that make them work. It is also a sourcebook for inspiration and organization.

The landscape designs presented here will give you general guidelines to plan your own garden. Look through them for the garden features that interest you, perhaps foundation plantings, ground covers, or play areas, and find one on a site that approximates your own. In the discussion of that site and its elements, you will discover the reasons behind the design and how you might interpret the design concept to fit your situation.

For example, in the section on A Sunny Slope (see page 64), there is a discussion of the way in which plantings of ground cover in a sunny hillside garden are arranged to relate to the surrounding hills. The key is a natural-looking organization of plants chosen for their color, form, and texture, which mimic the surrounding vegetation. Discussions of the maintenance requirements of the garden and the relationship of the plantings to the architecture of the house will help you to determine how well this design could be adapted to suit your life-style and your site.

## HOW TO USE THIS BOOK

Design is a process intended to create something specific to a site and the people using it. If you simply adopt a plan created for another site and other people, you will not only reduce its significance for you, but you will reduce the likelihood that the resulting garden will fulfill your practical needs. To use this book effectively, you should first understand the parameters that generated each of the designs, such as climate, soil, exposure, and life-style. You should also review the parameters of your site and life-style, in order to compare your situation with the parameters that generated the designs you like. Then use the landscape plans, not as examples to be duplicated, but as helpful suggestions in the process of designing your own landscape.

Each design describes the key elements of the landscape plan, revealing why the resulting landscape has the feel and function that it does. Feel and function are directly tied to the types of activities that the design accommodates, and these activities are also discussed. If the plan is especially applicable to your needs, you may want to pay particular attention to the discussion of the key elements of the design.

The book also explores ways in which the elements can be adapted to other sites. Since every site has innumerable parameters that together make it unique, it is not possible to interpret each design in a way that precisely fits your set of conditions; however, through careful evaluation of both your conditions and those in the design, you will be able to create a plan tailored to your needs.

To start you thinking along these lines, the book addresses the more obvious conditions, such as climate; environmental or ecological setting; lot size, slope, and exposure; soil conditions; the architectural style of your house; and your general life-style, such as whether the landscape is for a single person or a family, and whether you commute or work at home. To give you an example of how conditions affect design choices, a high-maintenance shaded perennial border on a north-facing slope may not suit your working life-style or your sloping but sunny site. However, the book addresses maintenance needs and more subtle design conditions such as the appearance provided by shade and the impact of slope, so that you can identify such conditions, relate them to your site and the personalities of those who will use the landscape, and then integrate them into the design process.

When you are ready to put your ideas on paper, consult Making a Landscape Plan (see page 18), which presents the basics of design drafting. Once you understand the basics, you will be able to draw up your ideas, revise and refine them, and ultimately either present them to a landscape contractor or refer to them yourself if you are installing the landscape.

The Landscape Plant Guide beginning on page 87 provides a list of plants arranged by category for each climate zone. So, if you admired an example of a patio with a small shade tree, surrounded by a perennial border and enclosed by an informal hedge, this list will help you select plants suitable for your climate zone for each of those categories.

*Opposite: The gently curving brick planters and path combine with the plant textures and colors and lend distinctive richness to this garden.*

# STYLE, COMPOSITION, AND PROGRAM

### Style

Garden style is really nothing more than a physical response to environmental and cultural conditions. Style usually has a regional quality influenced by land form, climate, and available building materials. Style also reflects cultural conditions, which are affected by such factors as religion, politics, and economics.

One style of garden that reflects the way in which these factors affect design is the relatively small, walled monastery garden of medieval times. Planted primarily with herbs, fruits, and vegetables, the monastery garden was, at least in part, a response to a hostile environment, a lean economy, and hilly terrain that offered few suitable building sites. By contrast, the expansive, meandering, natural English landscape garden of the eighteenth century, planted with ornamentals, reflects the gently rolling terrain, the benevolent climate, and a wealthy society that interacted with many other cultures and believed nature to be the highest form of expression.

*The strong, simple lines of brick paving, lawn, and foundation planting complement the house and showcase the mature oak while acting as a foil to the colorful displays in these flower beds.*

A new style is often a hybrid or an adaptation of an existing style. Styles overlap one another; precisely when one style begins and another ends is often contested. Our rapidly changing times, worldwide communication and transportation, and melting pot of cultures also make styles increasingly difficult to define.

However, an awareness of styles and the conditions that create them can help you decide on a form for your landscape. If your conditions match those from which a given style evolved, that style may be a reasonable starting point for the development of your landscape. But use that style only as a starting point. It is futile to simply repeat a historic style; unless a garden responds to the needs of those using it, it is unlikely to be a comfortable and pleasing place.

### Composition

A basic understanding of the principles of composition is indispensable in developing your garden and adapting plans to your specific situation. The main principles of composition are form, color, texture, scale, balance, rhythm, and focus.

*Form* refers to the shape and structure of elements within the garden. These should derive from and support the style you have in mind for your garden. Forms should harmonize with one another unless you wish to create a strong focal point, in which case a contrasting form can come in handy. A strong architectural form usually stands out, reducing the sense of its distance.

The *color* and *texture* of elements within the garden should also be harmonious; a sharp contrast in either will create a strong focal point. Keep in mind that insufficient variation of either color or texture can result in a fairly static setting, whereas too much variation of either can feel uncomfortably busy. A design principle to remember is that bright or light colors (red, orange, strong yellow, white), bold

## Creating a Landscape That Suits Your Home

When designing a landscape to fit your needs and wishes, never overlook the architectural style of the house. A successful landscape will be aesthetically compatible with the style of the house for which it was designed. In the discussion of garden features in the next chapter, each example of a landscape treatment is recommended as especially appropriate for a certain architectural style. Familiarity with these styles will help you design a landscape to complement your home.

*Italianate* and *French* architecture are the most formal in style. Houses of these styles are characteristically large, imposing structures that exhibit some degree of bilateral symmetry in the facade; that is, the left and right side of the facade appear to be identical.

*Palladian* architecture is similar to the Italianate style but is strictly bilaterally symmetric. It uses pure geometric forms, such as cubes, double cubes, circles, and semicircles; for example, a cube might have semicircular wings extending from either side of a central facade. All three styles often have pillars, French doors, bay windows, and possibly a porte cochere (a roof extending from the main entrance over the driveway) and a mansard roof. The building material is usually stucco, brick, or stone, and there is often much architectural detail and embellishment on the exterior of the house and related structures.

*Colonial* architecture is similar to but not as imposing or formal as the Italianate, French, and Palladian styles, although pillars are often included in the style. Monticello, Thomas Jefferson's home, is a familiar example of the colonial style. All of these formal architectural styles suggest a formal garden with strong geometric shapes rather than soft curves, or a strongly designed informal garden that complements the strength of the architecture.

*Tudor* architecture may have some formality and symmetry, but usually gives a less formal impression than the previously mentioned styles. Wood is often used on the exterior of the building in the form of siding, shingles, or the "half-timbered" look, in which masonry fills the spaces between the visible timbers.

The *cottage* style, which is less formal and symmetric than the Tudor style, reflects its English origin: a one-story stucco structure with a thatched roof and casement windows. Although the cottage style is less grand than the Tudor style, both are well suited to natural-looking gardens with irregular rather than rigid lines.

*Victorian* houses, often built entirely of wood and occasionally painted more than one color, are usually two- or three-story structures that are built close to one another and close to the street. The exterior details such as the gingerbread trim and picket-fencing are often carried into the garden and repeated on gazebos or summer houses. These are the homes of the elm-shaded Main Street of the past, with foundation plantings skirting high front porches. Garden treatments best suited to this architectural style have some symmetry in their layout and are somewhat nostalgic in feeling.

The *bungalow* style is typically exhibited in a one-story frame house with a covered veranda or porch on one or more sides. It has painted clapboards, or shingles that are either painted or left to weather; occasionally a bungalow-style house is stuccoed. This style is informal and comfortable. Appropriate garden treatments range from natural-looking to nostalgic.

*New England* architecture is most often illustrated by the Cape Cod cottage, a rectangular wood frame house of one or two stories with painted clapboards, or shingles either painted or left to weather. It usually has a gable roof, a central chimney, and the front door in the middle of one long side of the house. Appropriate garden treatments range from natural to nostalgic, although geometric shapes, perhaps clipped hedges confining a natural-looking arrangement of old-fashioned plants, are more suitable here than with the bungalow style.

*Modern* or *contemporary* architecture is characterized by crisp, clean geometric lines. It adheres to the design rule that "form follows function"; that is, good design results from thoughtfully configured functional spaces. This post–World War II style of building has large expanses of glass; long, low horizontal lines; and either angular or free-flowing geometrics. Although technology permits the use of numerous building materials in houses of this style, in many parts of the United States they are built of wood or brick. The garden styles that work best with this style of architecture reflect the geometric forms of the building as well as the configuration of the surrounding landscape, be it angular or undulating.

*Postmodern* architecture reflects a relaxing of the severity of the modern style into more detailing and decoration, with a sense of whimsy replacing the "form follows function" character of modern architecture. Elements from different architectural styles may be used out of context; for instance, a colonial window may be set into an austere modern facade. Garden design compatible with postmodern architecture can reflect this playfulness; elements from any garden style can be incorporated and the garden can be made either functional or purely aesthetic.

or large foliage, and silvery gray foliage tend to stand out in a composition and appear closer to the observer than they actually are. Conversely, fine textures, pastel colors, and deep greens create an illusion of distance.

*Scale* refers to the relative size of elements within a composition. A small tree over a patio feels appropriate, whereas the same small tree on a large boulevard will appear inconsequential. Think carefully about scale when you are adapting a plan to your site.

*Balance, rhythm,* and *focus* all pertain to the placement of elements in a composition. A fairly safe rule of thumb is to create a theme by repeating elements. This in itself can result in a pleasing composition.

If the elements in a composition are repeated at regular intervals to create a pattern, rhythm is produced. A pattern that is established parallel to a line of view or direction of travel encourages a feeling of motion. A pattern that is set perpendicular to a line of view or direction of travel announces a place of rest or a place to stop.

If the repeating elements creating the balance or rhythm within a composition are suddenly interrupted with elements of a different form, texture, size, or color, a point of focus is created. A point of focus in the landscape is a very strong element and one that should be well thought-out and worthy of the attention it will receive. Similarly, a rhythmic sequence that leads to a point without a focus produces a letdown; a composition with all balance and no focus can be monotonous.

## Program

The final requirement for designing your landscape is a list of features that will accommodate all the activities you wish to pursue in it.

*A strong sense of traditional New England is evoked by this simple front garden. The manicured lawn, boxwood hedges, ivy, and white picket fence are arranged symmetrically to convey a somewhat austere but pleasing approach to the house.*

This list, known in the trade as a "program," should include elements that will accommodate your considerations of how the landscape will be used, how you'd like to make it comfortable, and how you'd like it to look. Considerations of use may indicate that you need to include in your plan elements such as a patio, driveway and parking space, dog run, lawn, game court, barbecue area, or flower and vegetable beds. Considerations of comfort may suggest the inclusion of an arbor to offer shade from hot afternoon sun, a clearing warmed by the winter sun, a wind screen, a privacy screen from neighboring properties—any element that will make your garden a comfortable and relaxing place. Visual considerations may suggest a rose garden, a bed of your favorite-color flowers, sculpture or statuary, a birdbath—any element that offers visual enjoyment or stimulation.

A program is as individual as the people using the garden and their life-styles. Draw up your program carefully; it will help you to adapt a design concept to fit your needs.

## MAIN GARDEN AREAS

Almost without exception, gardens are composed of three main areas that can be defined by their shape and position on the property. These areas—the front garden, side garden, and rear garden—are typically separate, well-defined zones with little overlap, especially in communities governed by setback requirements. Even if the configuration of the garden varies from the typical, areas can be established that will fit into these categories.

For example, a house situated in the center of a rectangular lot with a driveway along one side has the three garden areas simply and clearly defined. They are the front and rear gardens, both of which are wider than they are deep, and the side garden, which is deeper than it is wide. A house situated in the corner of a similar rectangular lot has a wide side garden that takes on the characteristics of a typical front garden (wider than it is deep), whereas the "front" garden, although a point of entry to the house, may take on the characteristics of a typical side garden (deeper than it is wide). Some thought given to defining the relative areas of your property will help you organize your design ideas and make it much easier to apply the ideas presented in this book.

### Front Garden

The space between the front of the house and the street is typically thought of as the front garden. This space is usually small or nonexistent in an urban setting, medium-sized in a suburban setting, and almost any size and shape in rural areas where a hedge, fence, wall, path, or roadway may be necessary simply to define where the space ends.

Usually the most public part of a home landscape, the front garden can take on several functions and contain several elements. At the least, it serves to frame or dress the house. It connects the house to the land on which it sits with shrub plantings adjacent to the house (often referred to as foundation plantings) and provides a pleasant scene for approaching visitors and passersby. The front garden is also a part of the landscape of the street, the neighborhood, and the city, and

*The gate and the low brick wall of this front entry garden enclose a luxuriant array of plant textures, creating a delightful, private space that still says "welcome."*

*The generous setback from the street and the magnificent existing trees make this front garden ideal for a private patio. Large enough for a gathering yet intimate enough for two, this area is made welcoming with colorful plants, low brick walls, comfortable furniture, and brick paving.*

*The frequent landings on this gracious flight of entry steps and the zigzag route around clumps of lavender encourage a leisurely ascent from the street to the front door.*

thus has value to the community, although this does not mean that every square foot of land from the sidewalk to the front door must become public.

As land parcels become smaller and the value of land as usable space becomes greater, people are rethinking the function of the front garden. They are often putting it to work as a sitting or entertaining area; as a semiprivate entry court; or as a place to provide herbs, fruits, vegetables, and cut flowers for the house. If you live on a heavily trafficked street, you may choose to enclose the front garden to create a private space for your family and guests. Because the entry to the house is usually in the front garden, however, truly private spaces are difficult to achieve without some partitioning of the area.

If you enjoy viewing street life, you may want to create an area in the front garden from which you can see it. Benches, wide steps, and low walls are all conducive to viewing the street and its goings-on.

Whether seen from the street or revealed only upon entering the property, a front garden should be an attractive place. It creates the first impression of a house. It is one of the most visible parts of any piece of property and therefore should be given high priority in your landscaping scheme.

## Side Garden

Although on small house lots, the side garden takes on more significance, it is still usually thought of as a utility area. In its most typical configuration (long, narrow, and with little connection to the interior of the house), the side garden serves utilitarian purposes well. Since it is usually out of sight of the main parts of the garden and the house, it is a logical site for wood storage, trash cans, a tool shed, potting benches, boat storage, and so on. If your property has a side garden that fits this configuration, consider how these functions can be efficiently achieved.

If you do not need utility space or if your side garden does not fit the typical configuration, do not overlook it as a place to create special effects or accommodate special activities; the results may surprise you. If a side garden is well composed, you may find yourself taking your guests through it simply to share its beauty. A bench beneath a tree in a small space can become a frequented refuge from a house full of children or pending

*Above: This potentially neglected side garden has been transformed into a charming alcove by noted American landscape architect Thomas D. Church. Left: Often shady because of the nearness of high buildings, urban side gardens are perfect spots for ferns, babytears, and impatiens—the shade- and moisture-loving plants of a city oasis.*

*Top: An ample side garden can be used to exhibit favorite plants, such as the ones in this spectacular azalea and rhododendron "gallery."*
*Bottom: The sweeping curve of the stone walls and lawn in this shady rear garden is a delightful invitation to the rest of the space.*

chores. A side yard can take on new significance if it has flowering shrubs or vines whose fragrance drifts into a bedroom window, or if the yard is located off a bedroom and has a small patio surrounded by lovely plantings. Consider the side garden's size, shape, views, and relationship to the house and main garden areas before you fill it with firewood.

## Rear Garden

The rear garden is the space with the greatest potential and the fewest guidelines. Here more than anywhere else on your property, you get to make the rules.

The rear garden does not have to greet the public or frame the entry to your home, it does not need to accommodate cars, and it is not typically a narrow space out of the main view, like the side garden. Yet it can accommodate all of the uses and functions, and provide all of the beauty of any other garden area. It is just this lack of emphasis that can make the rear garden difficult to plan. To help orient yourself, review the Style, Composition, and Program sections of this chapter (see page 8). Then consider some of the circumstances and conditions typical of the rear garden.

The rear garden should usually have a strong relationship to the house. It is the part of the garden that is frequently opened onto or looked onto from the family room, living room, or kitchen. Hence, parts of the rear garden should be considered as extensions of the floor plan of the house.

Think about ways you use, or could use, these areas. Consider an herb, vegetable, or fruit garden next to the kitchen or dining room; a night-blooming viewing or fragrance garden adjacent to a bedroom; or an entertainment garden adjacent to the living room or family room. These "outdoor rooms" can also be used to handle an overflow of guests when you are entertaining. Regardless of the weather, outdoor rooms provide a feeling of space that greatly enhances the space inside the house. Let your imagination be your guide to think of themes for your outdoor rooms. Be inspired by your own artistic expression and whimsy.

Whether or not you choose to develop outdoor rooms, the view into the rear garden from the house should never be neglected. Since the rear garden is your space, it should reflect the personality of you and your family, respond to the architecture it surrounds, and provide a sense of satisfaction when viewed from the house. Perhaps you would like the garden to remind you of some childhood spot you were fond of; perhaps you are an enthusiast of the local flora and would like your garden to reflect this appreciation; perhaps you have a special building skill or artistic talent that the garden can reflect.

To keep the rear garden private, you may need to install screening, barrier plantings, or enclosing structures. The size and shape of visual screening should be considered carefully. To screen your landscape from an undesirable object, keep in mind the garden's proximity to the object. An 8-foot-tall hedge or arbor may provide virtually no screening of an adjacent

two-story building if it is placed far from the viewer and close to the offending building. The same hedge or arbor may completely hide the tall building if placed close to the viewer and far from the building.

When considering the use of visual barriers, carefully weigh the opportunities to admit and enhance desirable views, breezes, and light against the need to block undesirable views, sun, wind, or noise. A fence can provide a welcome separation from unattractive surroundings. And fencing may be necessary if you have small children or pets or need to keep out wild animals or intruders.

A well-designed fence can be an interesting, even striking component of a garden. It can provide a marvelous backdrop or support a cascade of flowering vines. It can divide your garden according to its areas of use. Consider using fences of various heights, patterns, and materials.

If fencing is necessary but visually undesirable, consider placing it just over a slope or behind existing plantings or structures, or use plantings to disguise it. In a formal setting, a simple row of shrubs may camouflage a fence. In an informal setting, random plantings of various heights can effectively obscure or reduce the visibility of a fence.

Keep an open mind when considering different types of visual barriers. All too often people put up fences where they are not needed. Depending on your setting, a surprising sense of openness and increased scale can be achieved by eliminating fencing. Hedges are another possibility. Although in the short term they may not be as effective a barrier as a fence, hedges—formal and clipped or informal and left to grow naturally—will eventually serve the same functions as fencing. A dense planting of a thorny shrub will keep in children and dogs and keep out unwelcome visitors.

In planning your landscape, try picturing your ideal garden, the visual qualities you find inspiring, the activities you would like the garden to accommodate, the special qualities you can bring to it. Then build all of those considerations into your garden design.

*The stately formality of this rear garden is produced by clipped boxwood hedges, a low brick wall, and matching jardinieres in a bilaterally symmetrical composition—that is, almost mirror images on both sides of an imaginary center line.*

*Whether your home is formal or a bit more rustic like this one, you need a fairly large garden to make a circular driveway appear in scale.*

*The basket-weave pattern of the brick paving and the crisply detailed rectangular wood planters integrate the driveway into this gracious, welcoming entry. The brick and the wood complement the blend of formality and rusticity in this contemporary house.*

## UTILITARIAN SPACES

Most gardens must incorporate functions that are not intrinsically attractive. A driveway, outdoor parking for cars and recreational vehicles, dog runs, and storage for trash cans, firewood, or tools are all necessary. The best way to accommodate them happily is to plan for them at the outset.

### Driveways and Parking Areas

Purely functional spaces such as driveways and parking areas are best not placed in plain view. In some cases, however, hiding the car wastes valuable living space. If the parking space is constantly occupied, try to make it unobtrusive. A dark-colored car parked off to the side of the property a good distance from the house may go unnoticed, even though it is in plain sight. (A car can merge into the landscape in the same way that switch plates on walls inside the house disappear.) Conversely, a red car parked directly in line with the house and in plain view of it will definitely be noticed. If you choose to block a car from view, a 4- to 4½-foot-tall shrub mass, fence, or wall will usually suffice. The air space above the car and the view beyond it will provide the needed sense of openness.

If the places for cars are seldom filled or are used just to drive through, they could double as play areas, with a basketball hoop or a game court net. They could also be surfaced with gravel, brick, or flagstone to form an open space in the garden or a sitting area, an entertaining area, or an entry or arrival court.

A home landscape will benefit greatly if the driveway is sensitively incorporated into the garden scheme. Bear in mind the size of your house and lot when planning this part of your landscape. A circular driveway, usually associated with an estate garden, can look out of scale on a small site. In such a situation it's best if the drive is not dominant, but is as simple and direct a configuration as possible.

Parking for a recreational vehicle is a critical aesthetic consideration because the vehicle usually occupies a space for long periods of time. If you choose to block this parking spot from view, a hedge, fence, or wall should be tall enough to conceal the top of the vehicle. You could join a hedge to a hedge that surrounds the property, thereby blending it into the background rather than calling attention to it in isolation. Since this type of parking area rarely can be adapted to other uses, it can be as plain and functional as need be.

## Dog Runs

Often as overlooked in the planning process as a side yard, a dog run in fact frequently ends up within the side yard because no better provision was made for either area. Unfortunately, a side yard rarely provides conditions ideal for a dog run—a combination of sun and shade, good ventilation, and good drainage. Yet these conditions can be provided in a relatively narrow area almost anywhere in the garden without depriving you of too much prime garden space or encroaching seriously on the garden scheme. Regardless of the size of the dog, the run should be at least 6 feet wide so that the dog can comfortably turn around; it should be about 20 feet long for a medium-sized dog. Ease of cleaning is an important concern. A smooth, hard, nonporous surface, such as concrete, is best; packed earth and gravel are not recommended. The surface should be sloped slightly for adequate drainage. Wire mesh fencing or ¼-inch-diameter aluminum rods, available from building supply stores, are sufficient to enclose a dog run; the recommended fence height is 6 feet. The fencing can be blocked from view with a simple screen of medium-to-tall shrubs planted between the viewer and the fence, leaving adequate space for ventilation between the fence and the plantings.

## Storage Areas

A side yard can provide ideal space for a storage area if you give adequate thought to movement to and from the area, and to the type of material being stored. Trash should be stored close to its source and the pickup point. Provide a bin large enough to house the trash cans, preferably with a lid or roof to shed rain and with doors if dogs or raccoons are a problem. The bin can be attached to or placed close to the house or garage. Its exterior appearance can be chosen to complement the detailing of the house.

Wood should be stored where it can be easily delivered and stacked, and where it is easily accessible. To keep the wood dry, store it under an eave or roof or erect a simple, free-standing roofed shelter.

Tool storage should be located in an area close to machinery, such as a lawn mower, and close to bulk materials, such as large bags of potting soil, bark mulch, and fertilizer. This type of storage area lends itself especially well to architectural solutions. A structure incorporating a tool storage area with a potting bench or a display area for a prized collection of potted plants is a welcome and handsome addition to a garden.

*Patio paving extended under a deck overhang or eave can provide a storage area that is dry and accessible.*

## Making a Landscape Plan

The discussion of each landscape plan in this book will give you the understanding necessary to translate the design concept to fit your needs. You will find ideas on how to make your landscape reflect your tastes and personality, how to make it accommodate the activities you and your family want to pursue in the garden, and how to make it complement the architecture of your home. Sooner or later you'll want to put on paper all the ideas you've assembled.

The process of exploring and documenting ideas on paper allows you to build upon an idea, let new ideas evolve, and refine your design as you proceed. Without a record of every idea—good, bad, and indifferent—it is hard to develop a concept fully. Your goal is to create your own landscape plan similar to those in this book, although you may choose not to use color.

Although all students of design can recall vividly their first encounter with the tools of the trade—an array of papers, pens, pencils, scales, triangles, templates, brushes, and erasers—these tools need not be intimidating. A few basic supplies, available in art and drafting supply stores, are all you will require to design a residential garden.

### Paper

Two types of paper are preferred for drafting designs—tracing paper and vellum. Tracing paper, often referred to as "trace" or "flimsy," is inexpensive paper that is sold by the roll in a variety of widths. Use this paper to develop rough ideas and to overlay and trace one idea onto the next.

Heavier, more durable, and more costly than trace is 1000H vellum. Since this paper is used only for drafting a final design, you may choose to buy it by the sheet. This 1000H vellum is reproducible; that is, blueprint copies can be made of the drawings on it. For ease of measuring, purchase paper with a light grid on it (typically eight or ten lines to the inch), which will not reproduce on the blueprint when the drawing is printed. This process is discussed later, under Reproduction (see page 19).

### Pencils and Pens

The conceptual, idea-developing phase of the design process is usually done with a soft pencil or a felt-tip pen on trace. The drafting of the final design may be done with either a pencil or a pen, and is usually done on vellum.

A wide variety of pencils is available, either as wood-encased leads (the pencils you have always used) or as simple leads, which need lead holders. Leads are graded according to their softness: A B lead is the softest lead, an H lead is the hardest lead, and HB and F leads are between the two (HB leads are softer than F leads). The B and H leads may be preceded by a number from 1 to 6. On H leads, the higher the number, the harder the lead; thus a 3H lead is harder than a 2H lead. With B leads, the higher the number, the softer the lead; thus a 3B lead is considerably softer than a B lead.

Regardless of hardness, pencils have the obvious benefit of being more easily erased than ink. Conceptual designs are often drawn with a very soft lead (2B or softer). A finished drawing on vellum is usually made with a hard lead (an H lead), which does not smear as easily as a soft lead and which produces a finer line, making it more suitable for detailed work. You may want to vary the thickness of the lines on your plan for a professional look worthy of your final design.

Felt-tip pens are the easiest pens to use for drawing. They are available in a wide variety of thicknesses. For finely tuned drawings you may want to experiment with technical pens, which are used for design drafting. They are graded according to the thickness of the line they produce, on a scale from 0000 (very fine lines) to 4 or occasionally higher (very wide lines). Technical pens are considerably more expensive than felt-tip pens and pencils, and unless you plan to prepare more designs in the future, they may not be the better choice. Bear in mind that ink is not as erasable as pencil and can be smeared as you work on the drawing. On the other hand, ink lines are darker and more permanent than pencil lines, so they will make a sharper print for the final design.

### Scales

After paper and pencils, the most helpful piece of equipment for drawing a landscape plan is an architect's scale or an engineer's scale, a ruler that allows you to measure actual distances directly on your plan.

The size of your property will determine the scale that you choose; most lots of ½ acre or less can be drawn at ¼ inch = 1 foot. Thus if you want to draw something 16 feet long in the plan (a line 4 inches long on your paper), use the ¼-inch edge on the architect's scale and mark off the distance between 0 and 16. You don't need to convert the distance to inches first. Larger lots may be drawn at scales of ⅛ inch, ¹⁄₁₆ inch, or ¹⁄₃₂ inch. You can use an engineer's scale in the same way. An engineer's scale is calibrated in tenths of an inch—¹⁄₁₀ inch, ¹⁄₂₀ inch, ¹⁄₃₀ inch, and so on.

The larger the denominator of the fraction, the smaller everything appears on the paper, so it's best to choose the largest scale that you can use on a reasonably sized sheet of paper.

### Drawing Aids

You can choose from quite a few pieces of equipment to make your drawing and designing easier and more fun. All are available in drafting supply stores. A drawing board and a T-square will make it easier to lay out the plan and draw straight lines. A 45-degree and a 30- to 60-degree triangle will help you to draw many of the most common shapes and angles in a garden. A circle template, with circles from ¹⁄₁₆ inch to 3 inches wide, will help you to draw individual plants and masses of plants. The landscape plans in this book use different shapes to represent trees, shrubs, ground covers, hedges, and so on (see Landscape Symbols on page 88). You might choose templates or even rubber stamps to indicate different types of plantings.

Drafting tape, one or two erasers, an eraser shield, and a drafting brush should round out your complement of tools. With these items, you will have everything you need to create a landscape design, from the rough, conceptual sketches to the final plan.

## Reproduction

Once the design is drawn to your satisfaction, you will need to make copies, either to give to contractors or, if you will be installing the design yourself, to take into the garden while you work. Although your drawings could probably be photocopied, this process usually creates some distortion of the dimensions.

Drawings on trace or vellum can be reproduced by a diazo process, which is more dimensionally stable than photocopying and produces either a blueline, a blackline, or a brownline print, depending on the color of the pigment in the paper. This process allows you to make an indefinite number of copies of your original drawing.

An intermediate diazo, called a sepia, is a reproducible copy of your drawing. Sepias are especially useful if you want to try different planting arrangements within one fixed configuration, or if you want to prepare an irrigation diagram, a lighting diagram, a paving materials scheme, and a planting plan for your basic layout. If a single drawing contained all that information, you can imagine how confusing it would look.

## Beginning the Design

Before you can design the garden, you need a plan that shows where the house sits on the property. If a site plan is not available, make your own sketch by measuring the house and its relation to the property lines.

To do this, measure the distance from each corner of the house to the facing property line. A house with four corners needs eight measurements (two at each corner of the house). Stand near one corner of the house with your back against the house, and measure the perpendicular distance from the wall to the property line facing you. Turn the corner of the house and measure from the wall behind you to the facing property line. Repeat the process at the other three corners of the house, making sure you take each measurement at a right angle to the house and property line. Transfer these measurements to a sheet of paper, connect the inner "ends" of the lines, and you've fixed the position of the house.

Don't forget to note on your sketch the location of any structures or features you want to retain in the new garden, such as trees, shrubs, or rock outcrops. Then select a scale at which to draw the plan. Make a base plan of the house and property lines that includes the structures or features you want to retain. You may want to do this on 1000H vellum.

Next, on a trace overlay make notes about the existing conditions, for example, the sunniest part of the garden, the shady parts, the areas that are windy or are protected from the wind, the low spots that tend to puddle or stay wet after a storm. This information will help you to decide the best locations for various activities.

On a second trace overlay, make notes about views—desirable distant views that you want to enhance; places where you want to block undesirable views or

screen your property from neighbors; views from inside the house into the garden, perhaps the view from the kitchen or the breakfast room. These notes will help you decide where to place the structures and groups of plants that will create privacy and shape the garden rooms. Just as important, the notes will help you decide where not to place things, so you don't obscure pleasing views.

Place a third trace overlay on top of the first two and lay out the activity areas for your garden. Do this schematically. Draw "bubbles" to denote entry areas and areas that will be used for outdoor entertaining, play and recreation, vegetable or cut-flower beds, utility and storage, and so on. The earlier trace overlays will help you choose the best location for each activity. Once you have a "bubble diagram" of activity areas, you are ready to start the design of your garden.

# Elements in the Home Landscape

*Let your garden design be inspired by these landscape plans. The discussion of each plan will help you understand what makes it work and how its concepts can be adapted to your site, the architectural style of your house, and your life-style.*

The first chapter has helped you define your landscaping needs; this chapter will help you visualize the most effective design solutions for them. Here you will find 33 landscape plans and accompanying photographs that cover all the main elements of home landscapes—examples of especially fine entry gardens, outdoor sitting and entertaining areas, play areas, swimming pools, ornamental pools, hedges, trees, lawns, ground covers, foundation plantings, perennial borders, and vegetable and herb gardens. The examples show a range of exciting possibilities, for example, a formal entry garden with double gates, matching clipped hedges, and a bubbling fountain (see page 24) and an entry garden that doubles as a sitting and entertaining area (see page 26).

Browse through the photographs and plans to find examples of the elements that interest you. Take a look at the discussion on how each landscape can be adapted to different architectural styles and garden settings. Read what makes each design work in terms of its function and visual qualities so that you can adapt the concepts of the design to fit your needs.

The plants in the landscape plans are listed by category, for example, low shrub and medium ground cover. The symbols on the plans indicate the number of each plant used and how the plants are spaced. See page 88 for a list of symbols. To find suitable substitutes for your climate zone, consult the plant guide starting on page 87.

*Placing the right plant in just the right spot can create a stunning effect, as shown in this perennial border.*

## ENTRY GARDENS

The entry garden is the most prominent visual element of the landscape. It is the face of the property presented to the public, and it provides the first and often the most lasting impression of a house to visitors.

An entry garden is usually most effective if it leads directly from the street or sidewalk, so that visitors parking in the street or arriving on foot don't have to walk around vehicles in the driveway to reach the front door. A convenient, attractive connecting path from the driveway to the house is always appropriate, but when it's the only comfortable access, the walkway from the street to the front door may become primarily symbolic or, if it is never used, omitted.

An entry garden is an ideal place for special features, such as a fountain or a piece of sculpture. A thoughtfully designed entry garden can also accommodate a sitting and entertaining area. Keep in mind that the entrance should be clearly visible from the main approach to the house, and the entry garden should welcome guests and lead them to the front door.

## An Enclosed Entry Garden

In this inviting space the front garden and the entry garden are combined. No visual or physical barriers separate them, and visitors are drawn through the entire space as they approach the house. Gates and fencing separate this coastal garden from the street and protect it from winds coming off the sea. Sheltered and private, the garden is a delight to visitors entering the property.

To temper a commonly held belief that houses should have "street appeal," with the house, entry, and front garden all visible to passersby, tour prestigious residential areas. Many of the houses in such neighborhoods cannot be seen from the street. In the garden shown here, gates and fencing in front of the house create a private, enclosed setting, making the area more than an entryway. The space is enriched by changes of level, raised beds, a seating area, and a fountain. The controlled color palette, based on plants with gray foliage, works well with the gray-blue siding of the house. The broad expanse of brick paving, with its curved pattern, sweeps the eye

1. Medium narrow upright tree (*Leucodendron argenteum*)
2. Medium narrow upright tree (*Melaleuca quinquenervia*)
3. Tall shrub (*Camellia japonica*)
4. Tall shrub (*Citrus* hybrid)
5. Tall shrub (*Osmanthus fragrans*)
6. Tall shrub (*Pieris japonica*)
7. Tall shrub (*Protea cynaroides*)
8. Medium shrub (*Chrysanthemum frutescens*)
9. Medium shrub (*Rhododendron* hybrid)
10. Medium shrub (*Rhododendron, Vireya* hybrid)
11. Low shrub (*Cistus* 'Doris Hibberson')
12. Low shrub (*Lavandula stoechas*)
13. Low shrub (*Raphiolepis indica* 'Ballerina')
14. Medium perennial (*Rosmarinus officinalis* 'Prostratus')
15. Tall perennial (*Agapanthus orientalis*)
16. Tall perennial (*Iris* × *germanica* hybrid)
17. Medium perennial (*Ceratostigma plumbaginoides*)
18. Medium perennial (*Cheiranthus* 'Bowle's Mauve')
19. Medium perennial (*Clivia miniata*)
20. Medium perennial (*Hosta sieboldiana*)
21. Medium perennial (*Pelargonium* × *hortorum*)

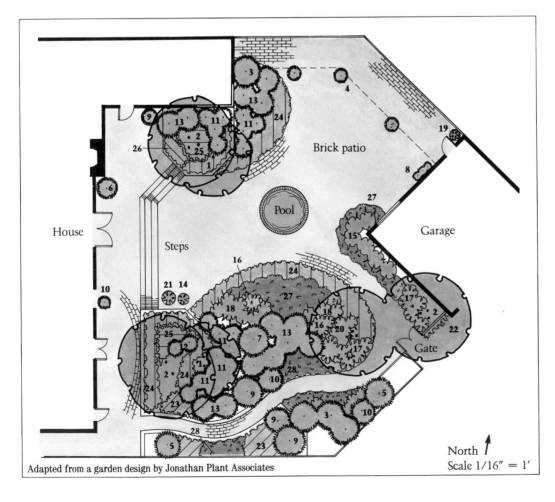

North
Scale 1/16″ = 1′

Adapted from a garden design by Jonathan Plant Associates

22. Flowering vine
 (*Clematis
 paniculata*)
23. Tall ground cover
 (*Trachelospermum
 jasminoides*)
24. Mixed medium
 ground cover
 (*Cerastium
 tomentosum,
 Stachys byzantina*)
25. Low ground cover
 (*Geranium
 incanum*)
26. Low ground cover
 (*Polygonum
 capitatum*)
27. Sun annuals
 (*Lobelia erinus,
 Petunia* hybrids)
28. Shade annuals
 (*Cyclamen* hybrid,
 *Impatiens
 wallerana* hybrid)

toward the house and sets the playful tone of the space.

This enclosed entry garden can be adapted to any terrain. Terraces can be used on a sloping site; raised or sunken beds will add interest to a level site. An enclosed entry garden is a particularly apt choice if you need to shield the entryway from prevailing winds, adjacent buildings, or a busy street.

The driveway should be separated visually from the entry garden with a fence or screening plants. The route to the front door should guide visitors through the garden without being contrived or circuitous. Paving choices include brick, as shown here, concrete, flagstone, cut stone, and tile. The entry should suit the architectural style of the house: The wide, flowing space in this example complements the ranch-style house, whereas a more geometrical space would be more appropriate with traditional architecture.

*Lavandula stoechas*

## A Formal Entry Garden

Formally arranged brick walls, double gates, and matching clipped hedges give a dignified, proper appearance to an entry. In this example, what might have been an overly dignified appearance gives way to a delightful effect as a result of appropriate detailing. The formality is moderated by the addition of tree ferns, weeping birches, and the gurgling, slapping sound of water from the fountain, which adds a touch of lightness to the scene.

The formal and informal aspects of this entry are carefully balanced. You can see on the landscape plan how the formality of the space is established by the alignment of the double gates with the front door of the house, by the symmetrical placement of the fountain in the center of the walkway, and by the matching brick walls and clipped shrubs. The formality is softened by the irregular groupings of the birches and tree ferns. (Although tree ferns are technically perennials, they are used in this garden as small trees and are designated as such on the landscape plan.) These informal groupings are appropriate to the setting because they reflect the asymmetry in the front facade of the house and the space in front of it. Since the facade is not bilaterally symmetrical, a perfectly symmetrical entry design might have seemed forced.

Formal or stately architecture is conducive to a formal landscape treatment. If you need to soften a formal effect, you might adapt some of the informal features in this example.

1. Medium shrub (*Rhododendron* hybrid)
2. Low shrub (*Azalea* hybrid)
3. Tall shrub (*Prunus laurocerasus*)
4. Medium shrub (*Loropetalum chinense*)
5. Large shade tree (*Quercus coccinea*)
6. Medium narrow upright tree (*Betula pendula*)
7. Tall shrub (*Punica granatum*)
8. Tall perennial (*Dicksonia antarctica*)
9. Medium perennial (*Iris* hybrid)
10. Annual (*Impatiens wallerana*)
11. Tall perennial (*Zantedeschia aethiopica*)
12. Tall perennial (*Hemerocallis* hybrid)
13. Medium shrub (*Fuchsia* hybrid)
14. Small pyramidal tree (*Prunus serrulata*)
15. Medium shrub (*Daphne odora* 'Marginata')
16. Medium shrub (*Acer palmatum* 'Dissectum')
17. Medium shrub (*Acer palmatum* 'Dissectum Atropurpureum')
18. Low formal hedge (*Buxus microphylla* var. *japonica*)
19. Tall ground cover (*Trachelospermum jasminoides*)
20. Tall ground cover (*Dryopteris diletata*)

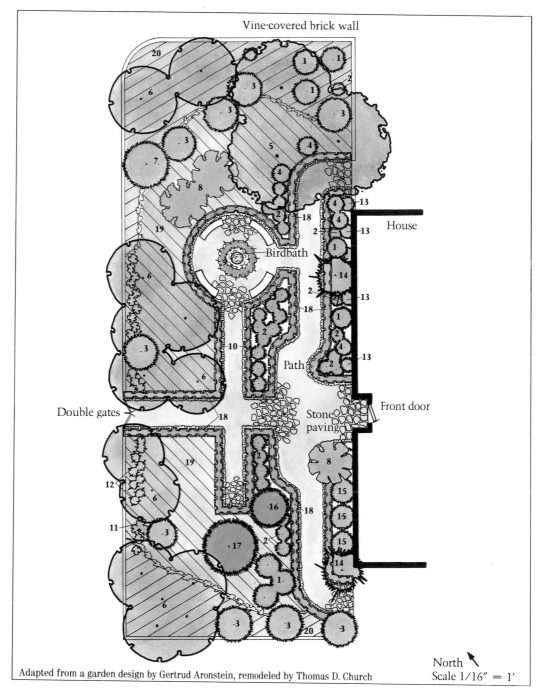

Vine-covered brick wall

Birdbath

House

Path

Double gates

Front door

Stone paving

North
Scale 1/16" = 1'

Adapted from a garden design by Gertrud Aronstein, remodeled by Thomas D. Church

Take advantage of the flowing lines of foliage and branches; the sculptural quality of plants such as tree ferns, especially when they're placed asymmetrically; and the random effect of paving materials such as flagstone. Remember that the sight and sound of flowing, splashing water softens the rigidity of a formal composition in the viewer's mind even when the water source is placed in a strictly formal position.

Although a formal style can be an expensive choice, it need not be. Arranging elements symmetrically costs no more than arranging them asymmetrically. The expensive materials associated with formalism—masonry walls and paving, and iron fences and gates—can be replaced with less costly hedges, gravel, and ornate wooden gates without a significant loss of formality.

Formal compositions lose their effectiveness on undulating land, so uneven sites may need grading or terracing to accommodate a formal scheme. Expect relatively high maintenance costs to retain the neat shapes of the shrubbery and hedges.

## An Entry Garden For Entertaining

This handsome entry garden plays a dual role: It serves as a private sitting and entertaining area as well as an entry—a practical solution for a small lot with insufficient space for separate areas.

The success of this area derives from the relationship of the fence and gate to the lush plantings. The gate announces the entry garden, yet it also provides privacy. The vine growing over it softens and incorporates the wood structure into the landscape. The fence and abundant plantings screen the garden and create a feeling of seclusion from the surrounding buildings. A colorful variety of plantings dresses up the space, lending it the significance it merits as both an entry garden and an entertaining area. The wood-decked entry walk expands into a large outdoor area for eating and socializing, with built-in seating, which makes it a welcoming and comfortable place. You can see on the landscape plan that the path to the front door is kept separate from the entertaining area as far as is practicable. Where they merge there is sufficient space for visitors to pass without interrupting the social activities.

The relaxed arrangement of asymmetrical shapes, overflowing shrubbery, and weathered wood decking suits a contemporary or ranch-style house. Clipped, symmetrical shapes and brick paving would be appropriate with Tudor, Victorian, French, or Italianate architecture. On the sloped site shown here, decking provides a level space. If formal paving is desired, consider terracing the site and building retaining walls to hold the slope.

1. Large pyramidal tree (*Cedrus atlantica*)
2. Medium pyramidal tree (*Crataegus laevigata* 'Paul's Scarlet')
3. Medium pyramidal tree (*Pittosporum undulatum*)
4. Small shade tree (*Acer palmatum*)
5. Small shade tree (*Acer palmatum* 'Bloodgood')
6. Small shade tree (*Acer palmatum* 'Roseo-marginatum')
7. Tall shrub (*Photinia glabra*)
8. Medium shrub (*Rhododendron* hybrid)
9. Medium shrub (*Euryops pectinatus*)
10. Medium shrub (*Mahonia aquifolium*)
11. Low shrub (*Cistus* 'Doris Hibberson')
12. Flowering vine (*Wisteria sinensis*)
13. Tall perennial (*Acanthus mollis*)
14. Tall perennial (*Agapanthus orientalis*)
15. Tall perennial (*Polystichum munitum*)
16. Medium perennial (*Pelargonium peltatum*)
17. Annual (*Petunia* hybrid)
18. Annual (*Impatiens wallerana*)
19. Tall ground cover (*Hypericum calycinum*)
20. Tall ground cover (*Trachelospermum jasminoides*)
21. Medium ground cover (*Hedera helix*)
22. Low ground cover (*Ajuga reptans* 'Purpurea')

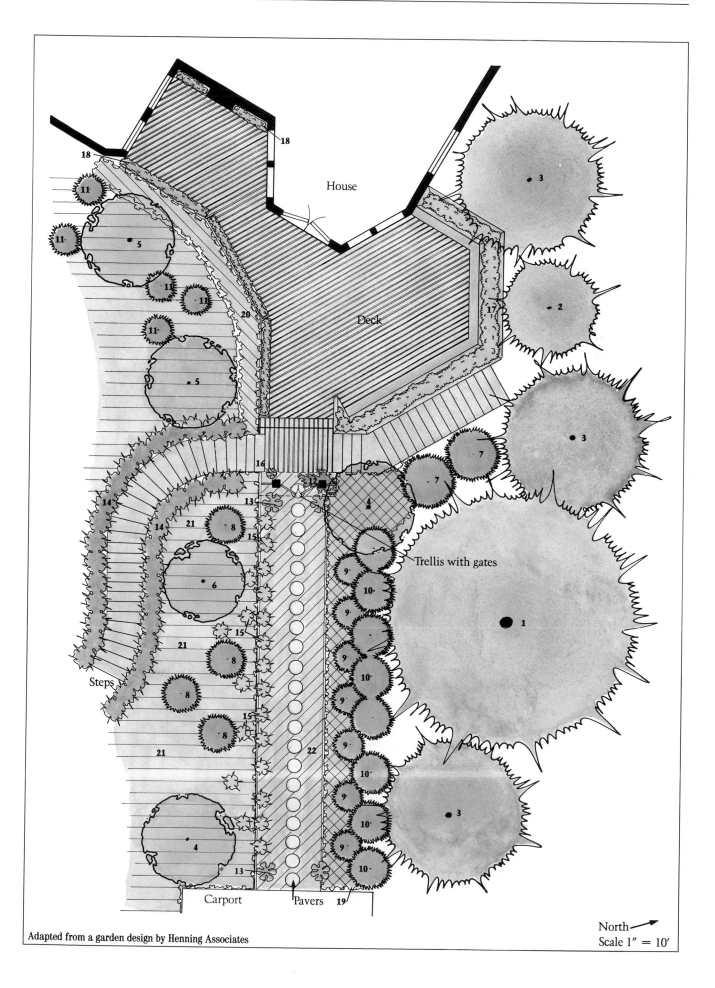

House

Deck

18

18

11

11

5

11

11

11

5

20

17

3

2

3

7

7

16

14

4

13

14

21

8

15

Trellis with gates

21

6

9

10

1

15

9

8

21

10

8

15

9

Steps

8

21

22

10

9

9

4

10

13

9

Carport

Pavers 19

10

3

Adapted from a garden design by Henning Associates

North
Scale 1″ = 10′

## SITTING AND ENTERTAINING AREAS

An outdoor sitting and entertaining area is always an asset. It elevates a garden from being merely decorative to being an integral part of the living space of a home.

Shelter and privacy merit the most attention when you are designing such a space. Protect the space from the elements and aim for a sense of enclosure that will define the space. Walls, fences, and hedges will protect a windy site; arbors, trellises, gazebos, and shade trees will shelter you from hot sun or light rain; screened enclosures will keep out insects.

Any of these features will also help define the space, making it more intimate than an exposed area.

On a small lot consider doubling up this area with an entry garden (see page 26), a play area, or a cut-flower garden. Bear in mind that the entertaining area should be easily reached from the house and large enough for the entertaining you may plan.

A sitting and entertaining area is a good spot for personal touches—art, sculpture, furniture, unusual plants, or a fountain. Let your imagination be your guide; this could become one of your favorite parts of the garden.

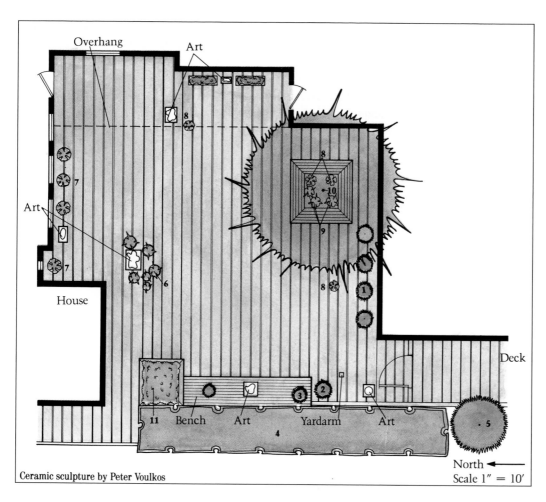

Overhang    Art

Art

House

Art    Bench    Art    Yardarm    Art

11    Bench    Art    Yardarm    Art

4

Deck

North
Scale 1″ = 10′

Ceramic sculpture by Peter Voulkos

1. Medium shrub
   (*Rosa* 'Iceberg')
2. Medium shrub
   (*Crassula argentea*)
3. Medium shrub
   (*Picea glauca*
   'Conica')
4. Tall formal hedge
   (*Cupressus
   macrocarpa*)
5. Tall shrub
   (*Phormium tenax*)
6. Low perennial
   (*Agave victoriae-
   reginae*)
7. Medium perennial
   (*Clivia miniata*)
8. Low perennial
   (*Crassula* hybrid)
9. Low perennial
   (*Echeveria* hybrid)
10. Large pyramidal
    tree (*Cedrus
    atlantica* 'Glauca')
11. Mixed annuals
    (*Impatiens
    wallerana,
    Browallia speciosa,
    Lobelia erinus*)

## A Deck for Entertaining

Imagine arriving for a dinner party, walking into your host's garden, and seeing this intimate, luxurious deck garden. The stage is set for a delightful party, and this area will undoubtedly be the center of it.

When you plan an entertaining area, keep in mind two important considerations—defining the space clearly and providing an appropriate surface. People feel more secure in a space that is somewhat enclosed than in an entirely open area; they're more likely to want to sit in a courtyard enclosed by low walls than in the middle of an open expanse of lawn. The entertaining area shown here is defined by the house walls and the large clipped hedges. The decking provides a smooth surface for the furniture and for moving about.

This space is effective for several reasons. The wood deck is compatible with the house siding, and its simple configuration suits the contemporary architecture of the house. The deck adjoins the house and is clearly visible from the living room; guests stroll comfortably between the areas through a glass door. Visual interest is provided by the variations in deck level and by the sculpture and the sculptural potted plants.

To create a feeling of enclosure on a raised deck, you might use benches or railings. On a deck built close to the ground, fences, walls, or hedges can be used. For shade on hot summer days, a broad-spreading tree or a trellis may be a desirable addition. Choose building materials that relate to the architecture of the house. The decking in this garden has been stained and allowed to weather naturally to match the natural wood siding of the house. A painted house may suggest a deck painted to match the siding or the trim. A brick or cut-stone patio is more compatible with formal, traditional, and colonial architecture than is a wood deck. Gravel is an often-overlooked option that suits all architectural styles.

Most decks require little care. Wood needs periodic treatment with a wood preservative, and gravel needs occasional raking. Brick and stone installed in sand may need occasional weeding, but installed in concrete they are almost maintenance free.

## An Enclosed Patio

This cozy sitting area appears to nestle into the house. The walls of the U-shaped house enclose the patio on three sides, making the patio and the house almost inseparable.

When deciding how to landscape an enclosed patio, think about the way in which the shape of the house will affect the design. Tucked in the area enclosed by this U-shaped house, the patio seems protected. If you were to place this patio in one of the wall junctions of an L- or a T-shaped house, it would be less enclosed, although it might still seem quite protected and part of the house.

Although the arrangement of the house walls largely determines the shape of the patio, you can modify the shape by judiciously placing planting beds between the house walls

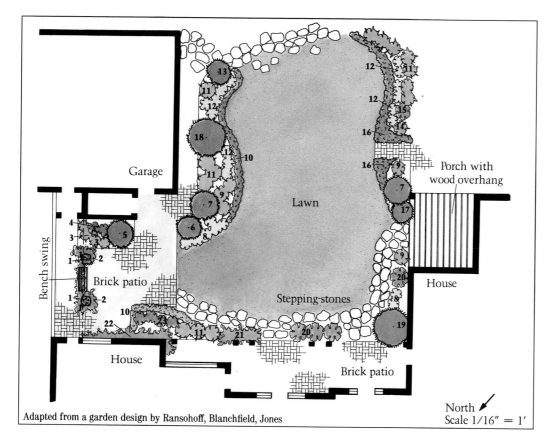

Garage

Bench swing

Brick patio

Lawn

Stepping-stones

Porch with wood overhang

House

House

Brick patio

North
Scale 1/16″ = 1′

Adapted from a garden design by Ransohoff, Blanchfield, Jones

1. Flowering vine (*Wisteria sinensis*)
2. Annual (*Petunia* hybrid)
3. Medium perennial (*Adiantum pedatum*)
4. Tall perennial (*Dietes vegata*)
5. Tall shrub (*Tupidanthus calyptratus*)
6. Medium shrub (*Citrus* hybrid)
7. Tall shrub (*Camellia japonica*)
8. Low perennial (*Iberis sempervirens*)
9. Medium perennial (*Coreopsis grandiflora*)
10. Annual (*Dianthus chinensis*)
11. Tall perennial (*Chrysanthemum* hybrid)
12. Medium perennial (*Felicia amelloides*)
13. Tall shrub (*Plumbago auriculata*)
14. Medium perennial (*Achillea filipendulina*)
15. Medium perennial (*Dietes bicolor*)
16. Annual (*Viola × wittrockiana*)
17. Medium shrub (*Gardenia jasminoides*)
18. Tall shrub (*Abelia × grandiflora*)
19. Tall shrub (*Chamaerops humilis*)
20. Tall perennial (*Zantedeschia aethiopica*)
21. Flowering vine (*Jasminum polyanthum*)
22. Flowering vine (*Bougainvillea* hybrid)
23. Medium perennial (*Anemone hybrida*)

and the patio area. Curved planting beds, for example, will soften the shape of the patio.

Planting dense tall trees in the beds will make the patio seem separate from the house. The beauty of this patio, however, derives from its strong relation to the house; the few low plantings allow the house to be seen and pull the space toward it.

This patio, roughly the size of a large room, is small enough to be intimate for just one or two people yet large enough to accommodate a few tables of four to six people for outdoor dining. If you entertain more people, you will need a larger space, but bear in mind that one or two people alone on a large patio may feel lost on it.

The success of this patio is due in part to its simple shape. Curved edges or geometric jogs could easily make a space this small feel contrived and would reduce its elegance. Visual interest can come from well-placed plantings, pots of flowers, furniture, or garden sculpture. The permanent swing on this patio, especially appropriate to the traditional architecture of the house, is an inviting place to relax, enfolded by the vine behind it. For a modern house, contemporary furniture would be more appropriate than the swing.

Paving material for an enclosed patio should be chosen carefully. Simple paving shapes are often most effective in a space of this size. Traditional brick is a natural choice here; it matches the brick of the adjacent wall, and it fits in well with the traditional architecture of the house. Cut stone, flagstone, or finely detailed concrete that contains a band of another material would also work well. For stucco or concrete houses, a simple expanse of concrete paving may be appropriate. A wood deck may look best with a contemporary wood-shingled house.

Since the lawn adjoins this patio, people may be playing Frisbee or turning cartwheels next to others engaged in more relaxed activities. To create more privacy on the patio, shrubs or a hedge could be planted at the edge of the lawn.

The ideal site for an enclosed patio faces south (if you live in the northern hemisphere), because it will be bathed in winter sun. To provide summer shade, add an overhead trellis or plant a small tree. A local nursery can recommend trees for your climate zone that are suitable for a patio—trees that do not cover the ground with debris and whose roots will not buckle the patio surface.

## A Garden Room

Truly a room outside, this latticework structure forms a private area that is especially appreciated in an urban garden. It provides a sense of separation from the house, from other parts of the garden, and from neighbors. This room feels less enclosed than a gazebo (see page 34) but more enclosed than a patio bordered by the walls of a house (see page 30).

The garden room is not merely a structure to be viewed from the outside; it is also a space to be experienced from the inside. The perimeter defines the space in the room and sets its tone. The architectural quality allows a choice of interior designs, just as there are different decorating possibilities for an indoor room.

This type of garden room requires a level area. It could be placed on a terrace, with the terrace wall as one edge. It could be placed dramatically at the end of a vista from the house or from within the garden, becoming the focal point of the garden. It could be nestled into plantings to make a secret room, or it could be constructed entirely of plants, like the space shown on page 56. The small trees and shrubs surrounding this latticework structure anchor it to the garden and make it look like a well-planned, permanent space.

A garden room is ideal for outdoor entertaining, so give thought to how large it should be and where it might be best placed. If you intend to use it for dining, make it large

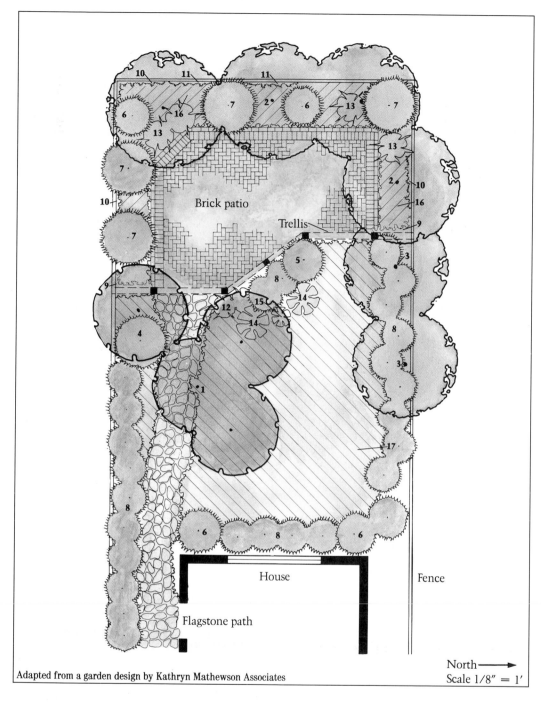

Brick patio

Trellis

Flagstone path

House

Fence

North →
Scale 1/8" = 1'

Adapted from a garden design by Kathryn Mathewson Associates

1. Medium narrow upright tree (*Betula pendula*)
2. Small shade tree (*Acer palmatum*)
3. Small shade tree (*Tibouchina urvilleana*)
4. Tall shrub (*Abutilon hybridum*)
5. Tall shrub (*Lavatera assurgentiflora*)
6. Tall shrub (*Mahonia lomariifolia*)
7. Medium shrub (*Osmanthus × fortunei*)
8. Low shrub (*Hebe* hybrid)
9. Flowering vine (*Wisteria floribunda*)
10. Nonflowering vine (*Ficus pumila*)
11. Nonflowering vine (*Parthenocissus tricuspidata*)
12. Tall perennial (*Lythrum salicaria*)
13. Tall perennial (*Nephrolepis cordifolia*)
14. Medium perennial (*Artemisia* 'Powis Castle')
15. Low perennial (*Viola* hybrid)
16. Mixed medium ground cover (*Erodium chamaedryoides, Laurentia fluviatilis, Viola odorata*)
17. Mixed medium ground cover (*Chamaemelum nobile, Eschscholzia californica, Laurentia fluviatilis, Scilla bifolia*)

enough to comfortably hold a table and chairs with room for guests to move around. Placed close to the house, it will be convenient to the kitchen, and if it is visible, it will entice guests into the garden.

Alternatively, this garden room is also ideal for activities that can be accommodated away from the house, such as children playing or adults quietly eating breakfast and reading a book or the newspaper. If you place it away from the house, you can more easily surround it with garden views instead of views of buildings. The floor of the garden room may be grassed, paved, or decked. If the room will be a dining room, keep in mind that it's easier to move chairs on a hard surface.

A garden room can be designed either to suit the architectural style of the house, or if it is visually separate from the house, to create a mood of its own. This latticework design relates well to a Victorian-style house.

Although relatively costly to install, a garden room like this one requires little more than an occasional coat of paint or stain and will return years of enjoyment for the initial investment.

## A Garden Structure

The privacy and shade offered by this small poolside gazebo draw people to it from the sunny pool area and from other parts of the garden. It is frequently used partly because it is placed where people gather.

Yet a gazebo may be intended to be viewed as much as used. This gazebo is prominently placed at the top of a slope (not visible in the photograph), with both the view up to it and down from it enhanced by the slope. Walking into the gazebo, the back of which overhangs the slope, brings you to the edge of the slope and a view of the lower garden and distant hills. On sloped land where you can create a dramatic vista, consider a gazebo like this one with plantings that block the view except through the entrance to the gazebo.

A gazebo that is meant to be used, as this one is, should be large enough to shelter four or more people. Seating is a must, and protection from sun and wind is desirable.

The design of a gazebo and the materials used to build it will affect the tone of the garden—how formal, casual, or rustic it seems. A gazebo composed of lattice and abundant detailing will produce a formal effect, whereas a simple structure of rough-hewn timbers will produce a rustic effect. One approach to designing a garden structure such as a gazebo is to make it reflect or complement the architecture of the house. Another approach is to build a structure, perhaps even a whimsical one, that reflects your tastes and interests and that deliberately deviates from the style of the house to draw attention to

itself. Such a structure can be just as useful as a more traditional structure, and even more pleasing if it is designed well. Let your creativity be your guide.

A gazebo can be equally effective situated unadorned on a promontory with a grand view or settled into the landscape with plantings. If you prefer the latter, consider flanking the gazebo with medium-to-tall plantings or placing it close to a grove of trees to make it seem less massive. In this example the medium-height perennials and the cascading vines help settle the gazebo into the site and screen the edge of the slope so that the view from the gazebo is a surprise.

A gazebo is an excellent means of achieving privacy from neighbors because it is effective as soon as it's installed, unlike plants, which take time to attain the desired height and density. Except for needing an occasional coat of paint or stain, a gazebo is virtually maintenance free.

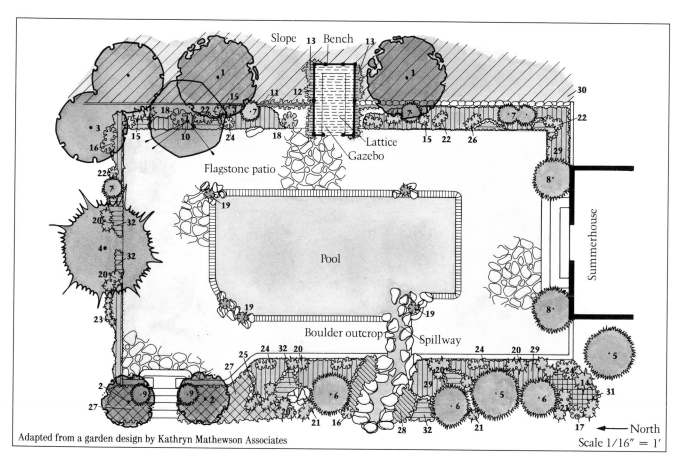

Adapted from a garden design by Kathryn Mathewson Associates

Scale 1/16" = 1'

1. Large shade tree (*Pistacia chinensis*)
2. Small shade tree (*Acer palmatum*)
3. Large narrow upright tree (*Phoenix canariensis*)
4. Medium pyramidal tree (*Sapium sebiferum*)
5. Tall shrub (*Arbutus unedo*)
6. Tall shrub (*Cordyline australis*)
7. Tall shrub (*Phlomis fruticosa*)

8. Tall shrub (*Solanum rantonnetii*)
9. Medium shrub (*Correa alba*)
10. Medium broad-spreading tree (*Olea europaea*)
11. Flowering vine (*Rosa* 'Tiffany')
12. Flowering vine (*Solanum jasminoides*)
13. Nonflowering vine (*Vitis vinifera*)
14. Tall perennial (*Hemerocallis* hybrid)

15. Tall perennial (*Iris sibirica*)
16. Tall perennial (*Penstemon* 'Firebird')
17. Tall perennial (*Penstemon* 'Holly's White')
18. Medium perennial (*Cheiranthus* 'Bowle's Mauve')
19. Medium perennial (*Limonium perezii*)
20. Medium perennial (*Santolina chamaecyparissus*)

21. Medium perennial (*Scabiosa caucasica*)
22. Medium perennial (*Sedum* 'Autumn Joy')
23. Medium perennial (*Tulbaghia violacea*)
24. Low perennial (*Geranium incanum*)
25. Low perennial (*Iberis sempervirens*)
26. Low perennial (*Nepeta* × *faassenii*)
27. Tall ground cover (*Correa pulchella*)

28. Medium ground cover (*Rosmarinus officinalis* 'Prostratus')
29. Low ground cover (*Cerastium tomentosum*)
30. Mixed medium ground cover (*Eschscholzia californica, Festuca rubra*)
31. Low ground cover (*Duchesnea indica*)
32. Low ground cover (*Stachys byzantina* 'Silver Carpet')

## PLAY AREAS

Child and adult play areas can be as simple as a designated part of the lawn or patio or as elaborate as a specially built environment with a game court or a swing set, playhouse, and sandbox. The value placed on a special play area depends on what other activities the garden must accommodate. It also depends on the proximity of neighborhood play areas such as schools, parks, gyms, and tennis courts, which may lessen the need for all play areas at home except for children too young to leave the house on their own.

The decision whether to develop a play area will depend on how well the area would suit your life-style, meet your needs, and fit your budget. To determine where best to place the play area, consider how it will relate to the other areas in the garden and how visible it should be. If young children need to be supervised from the house, the play area must be in plain view. However, a high fence surrounding a game court that is used by older children or adults can be more attractive if it is screened with plantings.

There are almost as many different kinds of play areas as there are people, ranging from traditional tire swings to tennis courts. A play area for children where their activities will not damage prized plantings and where their imagination can roam free will enrich playtimes. A game court to help adults unwind after a long day's work can be a wonderful indulgence.

## A Child's World

Besides providing a delightful space for children, a play area like the one shown here reveals the consideration the parents give their children. It is evident not only in the planning and creation of such a space but also in the play area's prominent position in the garden. Here, children's activities are a central part of the family life-style and thus of the garden created to accommodate it.

A plan for a child's play area should address considerations of location, structures, and surroundings. The area should be safe, in plain view of supervising adults, easily accessible from the house, and integrated into the

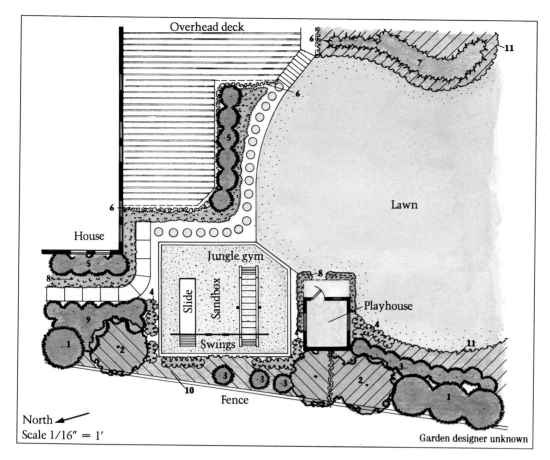

North ←
Scale 1/16″ = 1′

Garden designer unknown

1. Tall shrub (*Cotinus coggygria*)
2. Small shade tree (*Lagerstroemia indica*)
3. Medium shrub (*Cistus × hybridus*)
4. Medium perennial (*Agapanthus* 'Rancho White')
5. Medium shrub (*Abelia × grandiflora*)
6. Flowering vine (*Gelsemium sempervirens*)
7. Medium perennial (*Agapanthus orientalis* 'Albidus')
8. Annuals (*Petunias, Cosmos*)
9. Low shrub (*Escallonia* 'Newport Dwarf')
10. Tall ground cover (*Rosmarinus officinalis* 'Lockwood de Forest')
11. Low ground cover (*Cotoneaster congestus* 'Likiang')

rest of the garden. The play structures should provide enough diversity to stimulate a child's imagination. In this example, the play structures have been carefully chosen and arranged to create a rich environment. The beautifully detailed playhouse, with its shutters, planted windowboxes, and a front porch, is built to children's scale, completing their play world. A playhouse could be styled to complement the architecture of the main house or to resemble a gazebo or garden pavilion.

The surroundings are as important as the structures. This area has brightly colored flowers and an adjoining lawn for more active play. Flowers that are meant to be picked could be planted near the play area. Choose plants that combine enticing colors with scented foliage, such as scented geraniums or lemon verbena, or plants with tactile foliage, such as lambs ears. Poisonous plants, of course, should be avoided. A tree to climb and give shade might be a welcome addition, perhaps doubling as shelter for a patio where lunch is served.

Play areas like this are best placed on relatively level sites; but don't overlook the fun children can have playing on gentle slopes, wide steps, or low seat walls on graded or terraced areas. Seat walls, provided by the slightly raised sandbox in this example, are desirable even on a level site.

A play area should be comfortable. Ideally it will have both sunny and shaded spaces. If the garden has no shade, a tree can be planted; if it is totally shaded by trees, consider clearing a part of it for the children to play in. Children will enjoy the sunlight, and you will be able to grow a greater diversity of flowering plants and shrubs. Avoid windy conditions by placing the play area in the lee of the house, or deflect the wind by planting a hedge or windbreak around the play area. You can also provide shelter by building an overhead arbor adjacent to the play structure. Design it so that it can be easily made part of an entertaining area in the future.

Most people create a play area only if they have children of their own, but bear in mind the enjoyment it can provide when young friends and relatives come to visit. Although a play area is usually designed for children's use, adults derive pleasure not only from its inherent beauty but from watching children enjoy themselves in it.

# A Game Court

A game court is enjoyable for people of all ages. Teenagers and adults can play badminton, tennis, basketball, or volleyball. Young children can bounce a ball or play kickball, dodgeball, tetherball, or hopscotch. It is adaptable to a variety of games that require a hard surface, a net, or a hoop.

Give some thought to the kinds of games that will be played when you are considering a game court for the garden. Game courts come in several sizes, each designed for specific games and play options. The larger the court, the greater the variety of options. The largest courts are usually full-sized tennis courts (60 feet by 100 feet); smaller courts will accommodate badminton, tetherball, and dodgeball. Consult a court manufacturer or contractor to explore the size options.

Where to place the court and how visible to make it are important decisions. Convenient access to the court is desirable. Ideally, the access will be from related rooms in the house and adjacent areas of the garden, rather than from a contemplative spot or a formal dining terrace. The game court in this example has an expanse of lawn nearby, which can be used for play. Think about whether to screen the court from the rest of the garden. Here, the arbor effectively separates the court from other parts of the garden, although it does not screen them from view. In addition, the arbor provides seats for spectators and players awaiting their turn on the court. A court for handball, racquetball, or one-person tennis practice may need high free-standing walls around it, which would provide screening.

Three more points should be considered—the suitability of your site, the need for lighting, and local building ordinances. A fairly large lot is required for a game court unless you want it to occupy the entire garden. A relatively level area is necessary, unless you are prepared to build retaining walls and to grade a sloping site. Some court games require a high fenced enclosure; but before you install one, consider the visual impact and the local ordinances concerning fence heights and setback requirements. If the court will be used at night, you will need lighting. A lighting consultant will help you select the right type, number, and placement of fixtures, and will give you advice on local ordinances concerning shielding the lights from neighbors.

1. Tall shrub (*Photinia × fraseri*)
2. Tall shrub (*Myrica californica*)
3. Tall shrub (*Xylosma congestum*)
4. Low shrub (*Raphiolepis indica* 'Pink Cloud')
5. Medium shrub (*Abelia × grandiflora* 'Sherwoodii')
6. Large pyramidal tree (*Liquidambar styraciflua* 'Palo Alto')
7. Small pyramidal tree (*Citrus* hybrid)
8. Low shrub (*Pittosporum tobira* 'Wheeler's Dwarf')
9. Medium shrub (*Mahonia aquifolium* 'Compacta')
10. Tall shrub (*Viburnum suspensum*)

Court made by Sport Court®

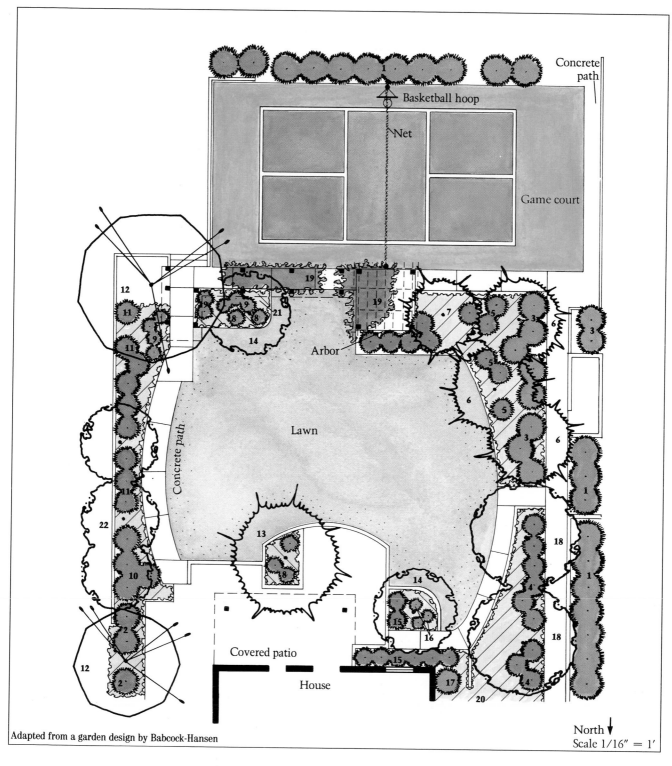

Concrete path

Basketball hoop

Net

Game court

Concrete path

19

19

12

11

9

9

21

8 8

14

Arbor

7

5

3

6

3

6

5

6

5

Lawn

3

6

22

11

1

13

18

10

18

14

2

15

16

12

4

Covered patio

15

2

House

17

18

1

20

Adapted from a garden design by Babcock-Hansen

North
Scale 1/16″ = 1′

11. Medium shrub
(*Prunus
laurocerasus*
'Zabeliana')

12. Large broad-
spreading tree
(*Quercus agrifolia*)

13. Medium
pyramidal tree
(*Fraxinus uhdei*)

14. Small shade tree
(*Malus floribunda*)

15. Low shrub
(*Raphiolepis indica*
'Ballerina')

16. Low shrub
(*Escallonia*
'Newport')

17. Tall shrub
(*Escallonia* ×
*exoniensis*)

18. Large shade tree
(*Alnus rhombifolia*)

19. Flowering vine
(*Wisteria sinensis*)

20. Medium ground
cover (*Vinca minor*)

21. Low ground cover
(*Laurentia
fluviatilis*)

22. Small shade tree
(*Prunus* ×
*blireiana*)

## SWIMMING POOLS

As a recreational feature in the garden, a swimming pool is unrivaled for its impact. Whether it is used for a cooling dip on a hot summer day, for an invigorating lap swim as part of a regular exercise routine, or just for relaxing with friends, a swimming pool can become the focus of a residential landscape.

To derive the most pleasure from a pool, place it in a logical spot in relation to the house, taking advantage of views to and from main rooms and the proximity of rooms that can be used for changing clothes. The sheer size of a swimming pool and its location near the house will probably make it the dominant element in that part of the garden. Plan its placement and design carefully so that you enjoy the pool for a long time.

If it is well designed, a swimming pool will be much more than a recreational feature. Depending on its shape it can set a formal or an informal tone for the garden. It can be made the focal point of a garden by adding a simple jet or fountain, sculpture, a change of levels to create a small waterfall, special edging or tiles, or planters with dramatic ornamentals.

## A Pool for Relaxing

The pool in this garden has been designed with relaxation and fun in mind. Unlike a more architectural or sculptural pool, this one creates a relaxed atmosphere.

The casual tone of the pool and the way it fits into the garden are due to its curving shape and to the deep blue-green color of the water, both of which mimic the surrounding vegetation. The adjoining lawn encourages play, and the lounge chairs and umbrellas invite sunning, napping, reading, and chatting.

The pool shape should relate to the general lay of the land and the terrain where the pool is being placed. The contours of the lawn and the outlines of the planting beds that surround the pool can be continued in the shape of the pool to strengthen the garden design. Even the shapes of distant land forms should be taken into account in the positioning and design of the pool. A shape as informal as this one may not complement a formal house or an extremely angular contemporary house, in which case the pool could be positioned away from the house and given a stronger connection to the surroundings.

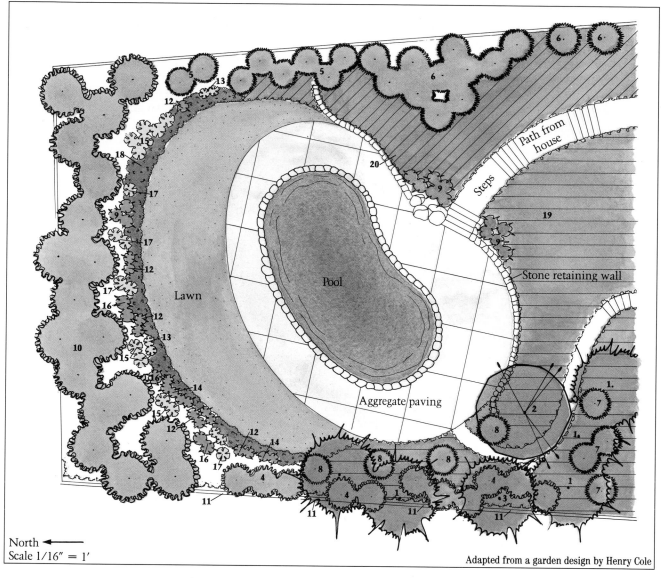

Path from house

Steps

Pool

Lawn

Aggregate paving

Stone retaining wall

North
Scale 1/16″ = 1′

Adapted from a garden design by Henry Cole

*Hydrangea macrophylla*

1. Large pyramidal tree (*Grevillea robusta*)
2. Small broad-spreading tree (*Magnolia grandiflora* 'St. Mary')
3. Large pyramidal tree (*Sequoia sempervirens*)
4. Tall screen (*Viburnum suspensum*)
5. Medium shrub (*Abelia × grandiflora*)
6. Medium shrub (*Choisya ternata*)
7. Tall shrub (*Escallonia rubra*)
8. Medium shrub (*Hydrangea macrophylla*)
9. Tall perennial (*Agapanthus orientalis*)
10. Tall screen (*Sequoia sempervirens*)
11. Nonflowering vine (*Hedera helix*)
12. Tall perennial (*Penstemon hartwegii*)
13. Tall perennial (*Dahlia* hybrid)
14. Medium perennial (*Salvia officinalis*)
15. Tall perennial (*Hemerocallis* hybrid)
16. Tall perennial (*Delphinium elatum* hybrid)
17. Tall perennial (*Nicotiana* hybrid)
18. Mixed annuals (*Antirrhinum majus, Lobelia erinus, Petunia* hybrids)
19. Tall ground cover (*Vinca major*)
20. Medium ground cover (*Hypericum calycinum*)

# A Pool as a Water Feature

The swimming pool in this garden illustrates how a superb design can also be functional. What appears to be a decorative garden pool is entirely practical for recreational swimming and even for lap swims.

Snuggled into the slope on a long terrace, this pool is strongly connected to the site. The design emphasizes the slope and terrace. In general, a design is more likely to be successful when it enhances a natural quality of a site. The pool pictured here is an excellent example; notice the way in which the edge of the pool on the downhill side falls away to step down with the sloping land. Notice also that the entire pool is tiled (as opposed to having a single row of tiles at the water level, typical of most pools), much as a Moorish fountain would be, a costly yet striking detail. The long, narrow terrace of lawn provides a simple foreground that does not upstage the pool. Pots of flowering plants add a pleasing touch.

When you are designing a swimming pool, think of it as an artistic feature—a water sculpture. Keeping in mind its function as a swimming pool, think about how its appearance could be enhanced by the color of the tile and plaster or by the addition of rivulets or

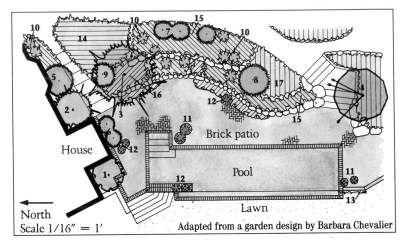

North
Scale 1/16" = 1'

Adapted from a garden design by Barbara Chevalier

spouts. Think carefully about how well the pool shape you have in mind will work on your site. Sloped sites open up dramatic design options—this pool is striking on its sloping site—but level sites need not be limiting. You can make level sites more interesting by building a raised spa adjacent to the pool, by installing another slightly raised or lowered pool, or by adding water courses or spouting water features. Level changes, unusual materials, and complex shapes can be costly, so be sure to consult a pool contractor throughout the design process. For inspiration look to ancient fountains, urban water features, and modern sculpture.

1. Medium narrow upright tree (*Taxus baccata* 'Stricta')
2. Medium pyramidal tree (*Chamaecyparis obtusa*)
3. Medium pyramidal tree (*Pittosporum eugenioides*)
4. Small broad-spreading tree (*Pyracantha fortuneana*)
5. Tall shrub (*Lavatera olbia*)
6. Tall shrub (*Phyllostachys nigra*)
7. Medium shrub (*Rosa* hybrid)
8. Medium shrub (*Taxus baccata* 'Repandens')
9. Medium shrub (*Camellia japonica*)
10. Tall perennial (*Iris* hybrid)
11. Tall perennial (*Pelargonium hortorum*)
12. Medium perennial (*Chrysanthemum × morifolium*)
13. Nonflowering vine (*Hedera helix*)
14. Tall ground cover (*Juniperus* sp.)
15. Medium ground cover (*Cerastium tomentosum*)
16. Medium ground cover (*Dianthus deltoides*)
17. Medium ground cover (*Hedera helix*)

## A Formal Pool

The classical Roman configuration of this formal pool looks appropriate with the stately architecture of the house for which it was designed. The pool is effective for two reasons. It fully occupies the terrace on which it rests, lending it an expansive graciousness it might not otherwise have. In addition, the symmetrical paving pattern and traditional pump house reinforce the sense of formality.

A pool as formal as this one looks most appropriate with formal or traditional architecture. The formal tone would be enhanced if the long axis of the pool were aligned with a significant viewpoint from within the house or with a main walkway in the garden. A formal effect is most easily produced on a level site, although a sloping site with terraces, as shown here, is also suitable. The less undulating the land, however, the better.

If the pool will be used for swimming laps, it is preferable not to have curved edges or steps at either end of the pool, since curves and steps make poor turning edges. Placing a spa in one of the half-circle ends of this pool would create a straight edge to swim up to, as would constructing the opposite end of the pool at right angles to the sides.

1. Large pyramidal tree (*Ginkgo biloba*)
2. Large pyramidal tree (*Picea abies*)
3. Medium pyramidal tree (*Betula pendula*)
4. Medium pyramidal tree (*Chamaecyparis pisifera*)
5. Large broad-spreading tree (*Quercus agrifolia*)
6. Tall shrub (*Acer palmatum* 'Dissectum')
7. Tall shrub (*Griselinia littoralis*)
8. Tall shrub (*Ligustrum japonicum*)
9. Medium shrub (*Hydrangea macrophylla* 'White Wave')
10. Low shrub (*Pinus mugo* var. *mugo*)
11. Tall screen (*Syzygium paniculatum*)
12. Tall perennial (*Pelargonium* × *domesticum*)
13. Medium perennial (*Catharanthus roseus*)
14. Low perennial (*Pelargonium peltatum*)
15. Nonflowering vine (*Ficus pumila*)
16. Medium ground cover (*Hedera canariensis*)
17. Tall ground cover (*Trachelospermum jasminoides*)
18. Large shade tree (*Liriodendron tulipifera*)

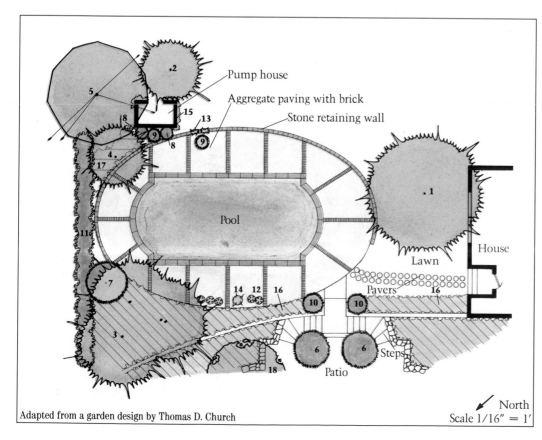

Pump house

Aggregate paving with brick

Stone retaining wall

Pool

House

Lawn

Pavers

Patio

Steps

North
Scale 1/16" = 1'

Adapted from a garden design by Thomas D. Church

## ORNAMENTAL POOLS

Water features are among the most striking garden elements. The sound of falling water or the stillness of a quiet reflecting pool captures viewers' attention and draws them to these delightful places in the garden.

A natural-looking pool or stream, with lush plantings draped over the edge, is the most appropriate choice for rustic architecture. A free-standing or wall fountain looks best with formal architecture, perhaps in a formal terrace garden. Traditional architecture is often complemented by a simple, still pool or a pool with a single jet or fall incorporated into a geometric garden.

A naturally styled pool can be constructed with a pond liner, or with clay or diatomaceous earth, which forms a bottom impervious to water. Formal water features often employ a tile lining or band and polished marble edging. Less formal water features often employ finished plaster detailing and rough-hewn or native stone edging.

In a naturally styled pool, plants can be set directly into the bottom, although invasive plants such as cattails are better planted in containers. Plants naturally found in wet habitats are ideal around a water feature, where they soften or conceal the artificial edge of the pool. If young children will be in the garden unsupervised, a maximum pool depth of 18 inches is recommended. If there will be fish in the pool, however, deeper water is needed to protect them from raccoons and birds.

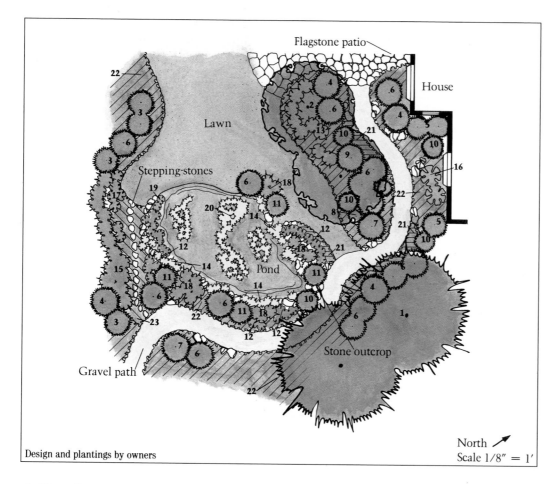

Flagstone patio
House
Lawn
Stepping-stones
Pond
Stone outcrop
Gravel path
Design and plantings by owners
North
Scale 1/8″ = 1′

1. Large pyramidal tree (*Pinus parviflora*)
2. Small shade tree (*Cornus florida*)
3. Tall shrub (*Kalmia latifolia*)
4. Tall shrub (*Rhododendron* hybrid)
5. Tall shrub (*Viburnum opulus*)
6. Medium shrub (*Azalea,* Exbury hybrid)
7. Medium shrub (*Ilex crenata* 'Glory')
8. Medium shrub (*Ilex crenata* 'Convexa')
9. Medium shrub (*Rhododendron* hybrid)
10. Low shrub (*Azalea,* Kurume hybrid)
11. Low shrub (*Juniperus chinensis* var. *procumbens*)
12. Tall perennial (*Dennstaedtia punctilobula*)
13. Tall perennial (*Hosta ventricosa*)
14. Tall perennial (*Iris pseudacorus*)
15. Tall perennial (*Osmunda cinnamomea*)
16. Tall perennial (*Paeonia* hybrid)
17. Medium perennial (*Astilbe* 'Glow')
18. Medium perennial (*Hosta plantaginea*)
19. Medium perennial (*Pontederia cordata*)
20. Low perennial (*Nymphaea* hybrid)
21. Low ground cover (*Ajuga reptans* 'Purpurea')
22. Mixed low ground cover (*Crocus chrysanthus, Eranthis hyemalis*)
23. Low ground cover (*Mentha requienii*)

## A Pond

Well-designed ponds, including this one, always seem settled in and a natural choice for the site. A successful pond provides a feeling of restfulness, an area of interest, and a focal point that draws the viewer's attention. A feature that can accomplish all of that is a powerful component of the garden, and as such its design should be handled with extra attention and care.

Creating an artificial water feature that looks as though it has always been there is a challenge. The surroundings should be carefully examined. Water always occupies the lowest spot in the landscape. If the pond is perched on a slope or burrowed into the top of a ridge or knoll, it is unlikely to look natural.

When you are building a pond, choose construction materials that match those found naturally on the site. The edge of a natural pond is much like the surrounding ground. If there is no rock in the setting, there is usually no rock at the edge of the pond. The way the land is shaped around a natural pond is also usually similar to the surrounding landscape. Sudden changes will feel forced. Simple pond shapes are best; sharply curved edges or too many coves and peninsulas look artificial.

Choose plants for the pond and its surroundings that make the pond look genuine. Plants at the water's edge are usually different from those found on the surrounding higher ground. Especially reminiscent of natural ponds are large plants with lush foliage that overhangs the water, creeping plants that form a ground cover at the water's edge, and plants with long, thin, grassy foliage that grow in the shallows. They will all help to camouflage the water's edge, which is almost never seen in a natural pond. Most well-stocked nurseries sell aquatic plants, and some mail-order nurseries specialize in them.

A pond that is meant to look natural requires much less maintenance than a formal pool, where clean, clear water is generally preferred. If the site has a low area, a pond is a good choice in almost any climate. Natural-looking ponds will also suit almost any architecture, but they are not often effective on small sites, particularly urban house lots, where a more formal water feature would look more appropriate (see page 48).

## A Cascade

The sight and sound of tumbling, splashing water is always appealing. Here the cascade rushing over boulders contrasts with the quiet pool at its base. Nestled into a low-lying spot in the landscape, this water feature is the star attraction of the garden.

A sloping site is crucial to the effectiveness of a cascade. To support the illusion of a natural waterfall, the water source should be concealed, and the stones along the water course should be placed to look random, as they do in this example. The weeping plants framing the cascade imitate those that grow naturally on the wet banks of streams, and the shade that the weeping plants and the other tall plantings cast on the sides of the water course enhances its natural look. The termination of the cascade needs to be well thought out. In nature a stream almost always ends in a body of water. A pool, such as the one shown here, is often the best choice.

Ideally the natural configuration of the land will make the slope for the cascade plausible, so that only a few stones or appropriate plantings will be needed to enhance its natural appearance. A combination of a cascade and a swimming pool should be designed carefully to avoid an inauthentic look. A cascade is compatible with any style of architecture, although in a formal setting it would look best if placed at the periphery of the garden.

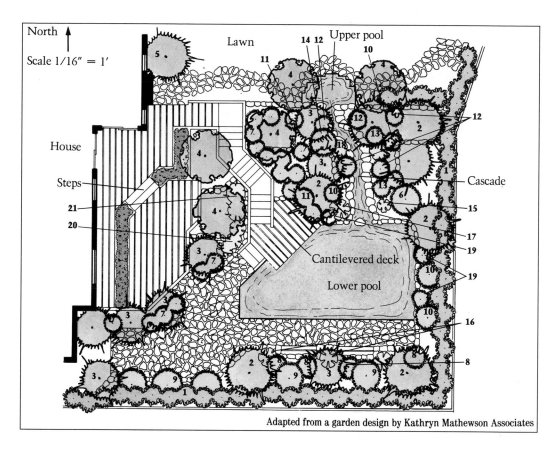

North ↑

Scale 1/16″ = 1′

Lawn

House

Steps

Upper pool

Cascade

Cantilevered deck

Lower pool

Adapted from a garden design by Kathryn Mathewson Associates

1. Tall screen (*Pittosporum tenuifolium*)
2. Medium pyramidal tree (*Eucalyptus sideroxylon*)
3. Large pyramidal tree (*Lyonothamnus floribundus asplenifolius*)
4. Small shade tree (*Acer palmatum*)
5. Medium broad-spreading tree (*Pyrus calleryana* 'Bradford')
6. Tall shrub (*Cordyline australis*)
7. Low shrub (*Pittosporum tobira* 'Wheeler's Dwarf')
8. Low shrub (*Ilex crenata*)
9. Tall shrub (*Azara microphylla*)
10. Medium shrub (*Abelia* × *grandiflora*)
11. Low shrub (*Hebe menziesii*)
12. Low shrub (*Ribes viburnifolium*)
13. Medium shrub (*Loropetalum chinense*)
14. Tall shrub (*Choisya ternata*)
15. Low perennial (*Erigeron karvinskianus*)
16. Medium perennial (*Mimulus cardinalis*)
17. Tall perennial (*Dierama pulcherrimum*)
18. Tall perennial (*Hemerocallis* hybrid)
19. Low shrub (*Rosmarinus officinalis* 'Prostratus')
20. Tall perennial (*Agapanthus orientalis*)
21. Tall perennial (*Alstroemeria aurantiaca*)

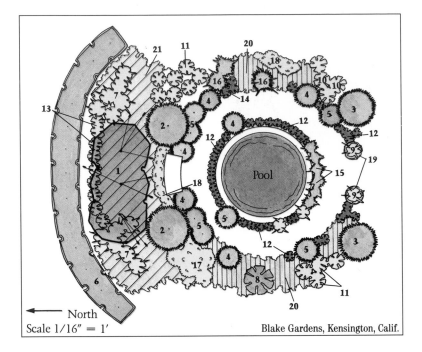

North

Scale 1/16″ = 1′

Blake Gardens, Kensington, Calif.

1. Small broad-spreading tree (*Citrus* hybrid)
2. Medium shrub (*Artemisia* 'Powis Castle')
3. Medium shrub (*Picea glauca* 'Conica')
4. Low shrub (*Santolina chamaecyparissus*)
5. Low shrub (*Santolina virens*)
6. Tall formal hedge (*Taxus baccata*)
7. Tall perennial (*Iris* × *germanica* hybrid)
8. Tall perennial (*Miscanthus sinensis*)
9. Tall perennial (*Yucca* sp.)
10. Medium perennial (*Erysimum kotschyanum*)
11. Medium perennial (*Helianthemum nummularium*)
12. Low perennial (*Iberis sempervirens*)
13. Low perennial (*Myosotis sylvatica*)
14. Low perennial (*Chrysanthemum haradjanii*)

15. Ornamental grass (*Festuca ovina* var. *glauca*)
16. Ornamental grass (*Helictotrichon sempervirens*)
17. Annual (*Calendula officinalis*)
18. Annual (*Tagetes patula*)
19. Annual (*Viola* × *wittrockiana*)
20. Medium ground cover (*Cerastium tomentosum*)
21. Low ground cover (*Duchesnea indica*)

## A Small Pool

The small pool shown here adds an exciting dimension to the garden. Although formal in configuration (the arrangement of the pool, plantings, and pots is almost perfectly symmetrical), a casual feeling is evoked by the rustic materials—concrete, gravel, and loose, billowy plants rather than the tile, brick, and clipped hedges typical of formal gardens.

This pool is at the edge of a formal garden, where the garden meets natural terrain. The combination of a formal configuration and informal materials is therefore appropriate. The circular shape of the pool is formal but less rigid than a square or rectangle. The use of gray foliage and yellow flowers is restrained and carefully orchestrated. The clipped hedge behind the pool reinforces the formality, while the small trees behind the bench offer a graceful contrast to the formality. The bench is welcoming and provides an intermediate level between the pool and the trees behind it. The contrasting dark and light green foliage of the plants effectively sets off the gray foliage.

Remember that a formal pool and setting are most attractive as part of a formal landscape and look best with a relatively formal house. This example of formalism with loosened edges would suit most settings; it could even be tucked into a wild garden for contrast. This pool would probably not work well with a ranch-style or contemporary house, although it could complement a traditional or postmodern design.

A simple pool is cool and inviting and can add a new dimension to a garden, yet it is affordable and relatively easy to build. Although small, this pool is appropriately scaled to the immediate garden; if it were placed in the center of a large backyard, it would probably look lost. A pool that is as compact and formal as this one lends itself well to entry gardens, courtyards, garden rooms, and sitting and entertaining areas, and it could be successfully incorporated into small urban and suburban landscapes.

## LAWNS

A broad, cool, green sweep of lawn is an image many of us associate with the good life. A lawn serves as an elegant foreground to a house and to flower gardens. It is visually inviting, and is an excellent surface for play.

Yet lawns are increasingly being considered optional rather than integral features. They require a great deal of water and considerable care. In drier parts of the country, lawns are often limited to play areas, for which there is no suitable alternative, or to confined areas where they add a dramatic touch that makes them worth the upkeep.

A lawn can be planted in all but the coldest climates. Lawns grow best in sunny areas, although shade-tolerant varieties of grass are available.

## A Sloping Lawn

On a sloping site where formal terracing is not desirable, a sloping lawn is an effective alternative. This gently sloping lawn, bordered by meandering beds of shrubs, reflects the inspiration for lawns—the rolling meadows of the English countryside.

The winding edges and the wooded backdrop add to the beauty of this lawn. Although the woodland trees are not essential, the contrast in height between the trees and the lawn makes the lawn look more like a meadow. The varying heights and forms of the colorful shrubs surrounding the lawn reinforce its natural appearance.

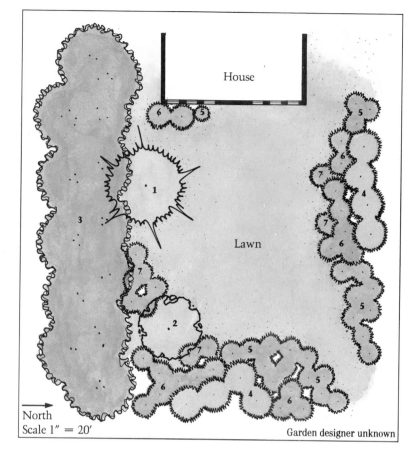

North
Scale 1″ = 20′

Garden designer unknown

Almost any sloping site can be planted with a lawn. However, the steeper the slope, the less water will penetrate the soil and the more difficult mowing will be. Since steep slopes are not as suitable for play areas and lawn parties as gentle slopes are, you may want to terrace at least part of the slope if you have those uses in mind (see page 52).

1. Large pyramidal tree (*Picea abies*)
2. Medium shade tree (*Cornus florida*)
3. Tall screen (*Pinus strobus*)
4. Tall shrub (*Rhododendron* hybrid)
5. Medium shrub (*Azalea* hybrid)
6. Medium shrub (*Rhododendron* hybrid)
7. Low shrub (*Azalea* hybrid)

## A Sweeping Lawn

For many people there is no substitute for a sweeping expanse of lawn, a style of lawn that originated in English landscape gardens as an attempt to emulate the expansive meadows found in the natural landscape. The natural-looking arrangement of the perennials, shrubs, and trees in this example gives shape to the "meadow."

This lawn succeeds because of its natural configuration; it curves graciously with the gentle undulations of the land. Tight, contrived curves in small spaces will spoil the natural effect. The impression of a meadow is enhanced by surrounding the lawn with taller plantings, especially woodland trees. To open up a view or to promote an illusion of distance, you might design the lawn to disappear over a slope or around a corner. An expansive, meadowlike lawn is most appropriate in areas where grassy meadows occur naturally or at least where the surroundings have a similar quality, such as an open field, so that the lawn harmonizes with the rest of the landscape.

Lawns require exceptional amounts of water and, therefore, are best suited to the northern Midwest, the Pacific Northwest, and the East Coast. Most turfgrasses prefer full sun, although some will tolerate light shade or shade during part of the day. A level or slightly undulating site is preferable, but a lawn may be grown on a slope if it is gentle enough to be mowed and to permit sufficient water absorption. A sweeping lawn will look right with most architectural styles, although a geometric configuration would be better suited to extremely formal architecture.

For optimum growth, turfgrasses need deep, relatively rich soil and require mowing, edging, fertilizing, aerating, weeding, and watering. Lawns are among the most costly garden features to maintain, but if you've set your heart on a lawn, the time and money may be well spent.

1. Tall shrub (*Eucryphia* × *nymansensis*)
2. Medium shrub (*Rhododendron augustinii* 'Electra')
3. Low shrub (*Hebe menziesii*)
4. Medium shrub (*Ribes sanguineum*)
5. Medium shrub (*Rhododendron* × *forsteranum*)
6. Medium perennial (*Nepeta* × *faassenii*)
7. Tall perennial (*Helleborus lividus corsicus*)
8. Low shrub (*Rhododendron* 'Blue Diamond')
9. Tall shrub (*Stachyurus praecox*)
10. Medium shrub (*Camellia sasanqua* 'White Doves')
11. Medium shrub (*Camellia sasanqua* 'Hana Jiman')
12. Large pyramidal tree (*Sequoia sempervirens*)
13. Medium perennial (*Brunnera macrophylla*)
14. Medium shrub (*Rhododendron* 'Trude Webster')
15. Small shade tree (*Acer palmatum*)
16. Medium shrub (*Rhododendron* 'Rose Scott')
17. Large pyramidal tree (*Cedrus atlantica*)
18. Small shade tree (*Acer circinatum*)
19. Small broad-spreading tree (*Magnolia* × *soulangiana*)
20. Low perennial (*Iberis sempervirens*)
21. Annual (*Lobelia erinus*)
22. Medium ground cover (*Vinca minor*)

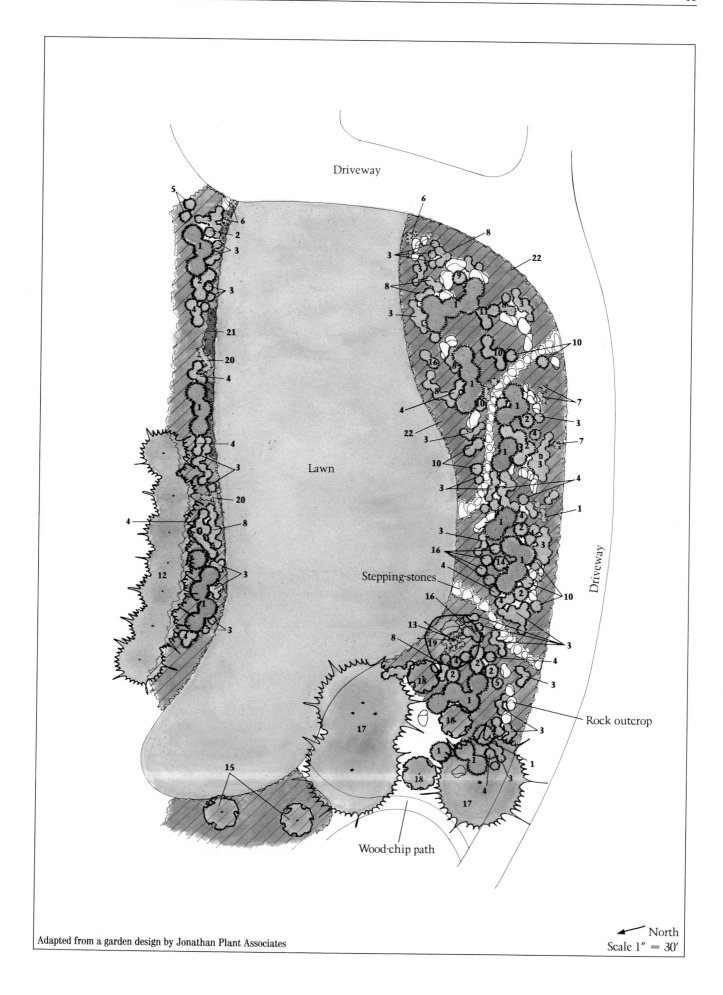

Driveway

Lawn

Stepping-stones

Driveway

Rock outcrop

Wood-chip path

Adapted from a garden design by Jonathan Plant Associates

North
Scale 1″ = 30′

## A Terraced Lawn

Terraced gardens are not new; the idea dates back to early Italian gardens. In this example a sloping site has been graded into level terraces with short but very steep slopes and retaining walls between them, and the terraces have been grassed. This is one way to place lawns on a sloping site; the other is to let the lawns follow the natural lay of the land, which is possible on a slope less steep than this one (see page 49).

Terracing a slope to plant lawns has both advantages and disadvantages. Terraces divide a space, which may or may not be desirable. Here, terracing provides a lawn for children's play and a lawn for adult use. Terracing can be an ideal way to divide a lawn into distinct activity areas and to provide a

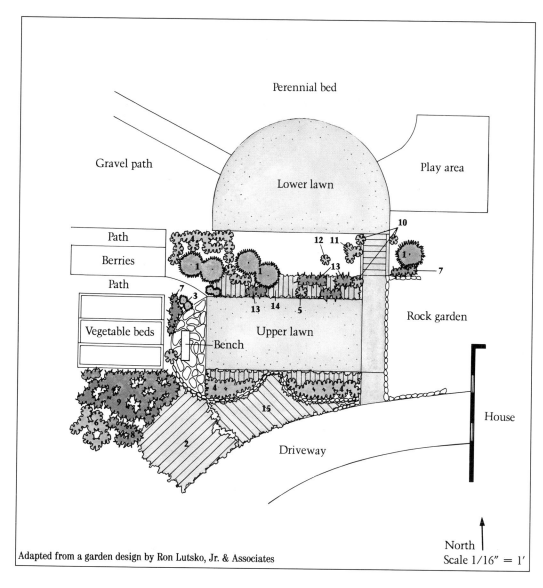

Perennial bed

Gravel path

Lower lawn

Play area

Path

Berries

Path

Vegetable beds

Bench

Upper lawn

Rock garden

House

Driveway

North
Scale 1/16″ = 1′

Adapted from a garden design by Ron Lutsko, Jr. & Associates

1. Medium shrub
(*Artemisia* 'Powis Castle')
2. Low ground cover
(*Arctostaphylos uva-ursi*)
3. Low shrub
(*Lavandula* 'Hidcote')
4. Tall perennial
(*Penstemon* 'Huntington Pink')
5. Medium perennial
(*Eschscholzia californica*)
6. Medium perennial
(*Helichrysum* sp.)
7. Low perennial
(*Heuchera sanguinea* 'Lillian's Pink')
8. Medium perennial
(*Iris* 'Victoria Falls')
9. Medium perennial
(*Penstemon heterophyllus*)
10. Low perennial
(*Erigeron* × 'Moerheimii')
11. Low perennial
(*Eriogonum umbellatum*)
12. Low perennial
(*Phlox douglasii*)
13. Low perennial
(*Salvia officinalis* 'Purpurea')
14. Low ground cover
(*Stachys byzantina* 'Silver Carpet')
15. Medium ground cover (*Iris*, Pacific Coast hybrids)

restful, private place away from the bustle of children playing. Terracing creates level areas out of less usable steeply sloped areas. And terracing controls runoff—more water will penetrate the soil on a terrace than on a slope. This is especially important during a drought.

The disadvantages of terracing are that it reduces the square footage of each area by dividing the space and that it can be expensive to install.

On the site illustrated here, the sizes of the terraces are sufficient for the play and sitting areas, and the terracing provides a welcome visual break as you look down a long, narrow portion of the lot.

Terracing can give the illusion of greater distance, especially if the farthest terrace is partially or fully hidden from view. The effectiveness of the illusion depends on the size of the space, the degree of the slope, and the

perspective of the viewer. When a long, moderate slope is viewed from above, as pictured here, a sense of greater distance is created by revealing just a hint of the lower terrace. Were this a short, steep site with an unobstructed view of the lower terrace, an unwelcome foreshortening would occur because the eye would be led directly to the flat area below. However, when a slope is viewed from below, and the top of the site is above the viewer, an illusion of distance is created because the upper terrace disappears from sight. Carefully consider these illusion-of-distance effects when you are designing a lawn on a sloping site.

Terraced lawns are appropriate for a wide variety of sloped settings and are easier to mow and trim than are sloping lawns. They are especially well suited to formal gardens.

## SCREENS AND HEDGES

A hedge is one of the most useful elements in a garden. It can provide the physical framework of the garden, controlling what is seen and not seen. It is ideal for screening an untidy children's play area or the less-than-manicured appearance of a vegetable or cutting garden. It can define spaces for different activities, and it can direct people through a garden. A hedge can even replace walls and fences, although patience is needed while the plants reach their mature size and form. A hedge can frame beds of other plants or it can be the main component of a design, as it is in the parterre garden (see page 58).

A dense planting of thorny or spiny plants can be as effective a barrier as barbed wire. Tall rows of evergreen plants, set close together, can block unwanted views into or out of a property and can reduce or redirect undesirable winds. They can also be used to create outdoor rooms open to the sky (see page 56). Low hedges can screen unsightly elements in the foreground while keeping open a delightful distant view.

When you are choosing between a formal and an informal hedge, remember that finely textured plants clipped to a clean, architectural outline are characteristic of formal gardens and will impart a formal quality to a space. They will also require a fair amount of care. A hedge composed of coarser-textured plants allowed to assume a softer outline will impart a more informal tone and may need almost no care.

### An Informal Hedge

One of the primary functions of a hedgerow is to provide screening. An informal row of shrubs can ensure privacy from a street or an adjacent building, block an undesirable view, or separate areas within a garden to accommodate various activities or different effects.

Depending on the hedging plants used, a variety of effects can be achieved. Some plants produce a loose, billowy effect, whereas others, such as the boxwood shown here, look more refined due to their fine texture and regular outline. This traditional hedge planting nicely complements the traditional clapboard house and brick driveway.

Determine what kind of hedge would fit in with the style of your garden and what the

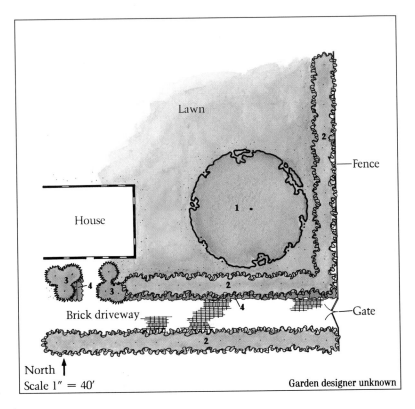

Lawn

House

Fence

3

4

3

Brick driveway

Gate

North

Scale 1″ = 40′

Garden designer unknown

hedge must screen. You may wish to block a neighbor's roof line while preserving a view of the ridge beyond, or you may want to enclose a children's play area or screen a parking area.

Carefully consider the hedge height you need to achieve the desired amount of screening. The height of the hedge shown here is right for the situation. Imagine yourself in the garden next to the house; the hedge is high enough to block the view into the garden from the driveway but low enough to allow a view above and beyond it.

Height becomes more critical on a sloping site. If the object you want to screen is down the slope, the plants will need to be much taller than if it were up the slope. Think over the qualities the screen should have. If you want the hedgerow to be showy, select flowering shrubs, shrubs of interesting form, or perhaps a combination of several species of plants for variety. For a list of flowering shrubs and informal hedges that will do well in your landscape, see the plants designated (F) under the appropriate climate zone in the plant guide starting on page 87. If you prefer a neutral backdrop or foreground, select a screening plant that looks uniform. Formal gardens look best with a simple hedge that has a fairly even outline, whereas less formal settings call for plants with a looser growth habit.

1. Large shade tree (*Acer saccharinum*)
2. Medium screen (*Buxus sempervirens*)
3. Medium shrub (*Rhododendron* hybrid)
4. Medium ground cover (*Hedera helix* 'Baltica')

## Living Architecture

Well-clipped hedges function as walls in this landscape, creating a beguiling outdoor room.

At different points in the history of landscape gardening, it has been fashionable to train plants into a variety of shapes, from simple geometric forms to elaborate curves and imitations of animals and furniture. The most frequently seen shape, however, is that of a tightly clipped linear hedge, such as the one shown here. Since hedges are used primarily to create walls that both screen the surroundings and define a space, they are a choice building material for garden rooms open to the sky.

The room in this example is a fairly literal translation of that idea. Located at the opposite end of the property from the house, the room creates an architectural anchor to balance the house; a more natural garden is situated in between. The tall, architecturally sculpted hedges create the required structure of the outdoor room. The decorations are plain—a few pieces of furniture, a green wall-to-wall "carpet," and a sculptural tree framed in boxwood. A few well-placed perennials could be added for color.

Whether or not you wish to be this literal, using a hedge to create an outdoor room has wide applications. The tables and chairs in the example suggest the room's suitability as an entertaining area. The room has often been used for weddings and in fact is called the "wedding garden" by its owner. The space could also be a secret room with which to surprise and delight guests. The sense of enclosure and privacy makes such an area ideal for a garden off a bedroom or as a quiet escape for reading or contemplation.

A literal interpretation of the clipped hedge–enclosed room idea produces a formal effect, whereas less literal interpretations—unclipped hedges, irregular shapes, open-ended spaces—suit a more relaxed life-style and less formal architecture. In either case a hedge-enclosed room is an effective solution for a site with no privacy, too much wind, or an undesirable view. You might even like to copy the Italian gardens and create a series of hedge-enclosed rooms, each with its own character. Keep in mind that hedging plants vary in their rate of growth. If you choose fast-growing plants, the room will take shape more quickly, but it will require more care.

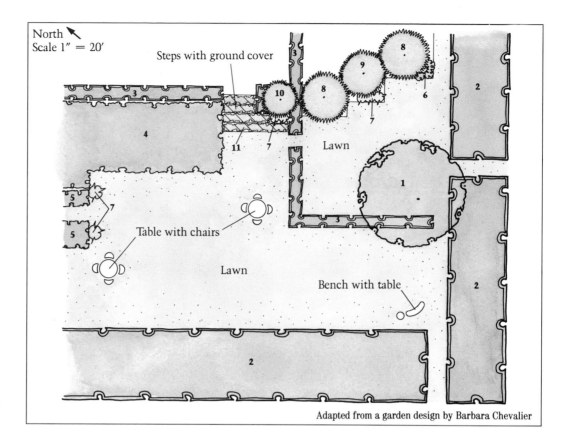

North
Scale 1″ = 20′

Steps with ground cover

3

8

9

10

8

6

2

4

11    7

7

Lawn

3

1

5

7

Table with chairs

5

Lawn

Bench with table

2

2

Adapted from a garden design by Barbara Chevalier

*Below: Hydrangeas and gladioluses thrive in the naturally planted garden area between the house and the outdoor room.*

1. Small shade tree (*Malus floribunda*)
2. Tall formal hedge (*Cupressus macrocarpa*)
3. Medium formal hedge (*Buxus microphylla* var. *japonica*)
4. Informal hedge (*Bambusa glaucescens*)
5. Informal hedge (*Rosa eglanteria*)
6. Medium perennial (*Iris xiphium* hybrid)
7. Medium perennial (*Crocosmia masoniorum*)
8. Tall shrub (*Ilex aquifolium*)
9. Tall shrub (*Ilex aquifolium* 'Aureo-marginata')
10. Medium shrub (*Juniperus chinensis* 'Pfitzerana')
11. Low ground cover (*Laurentia fluviatilis*)

# A Parterre

Derived from the historic gardens of Europe, the parterre still has application in modern formal gardens. The word *parterre* in a gardening context refers to geometrically shaped beds in a landscape. The beds can be any shape or size and are typically used in formal compositions. The highest expression of the parterre was achieved on large French estates, where elaborate patterns of curves, swirls, paisleys, arabesques, rectangles, and squares were symmetrically arranged.

In this garden, hedges create the parterres. They are not being used to screen or to define activity areas, but to define planting areas that have a purely decorative function.

This example of a true parterre—one that is perfectly balanced—has four simple elements: brick paving, low boxwood hedges, roses, and a citrus tree. The symmetrical arrangement and clean lines of the brick and hedge compose the formal structure. The roses and citrus, although symmetrically arranged, are irregular in form and break the stiffness in the formal layout. This contrast between soft, informal plantings and geometric low hedges is often used to achieve delightful effects in a parterre garden.

Traditionally, parterres are filled with geraniums, Siberian iris, lavender, roses (as shown here), or annuals. The low hedges are most frequently boxwood, although dwarf

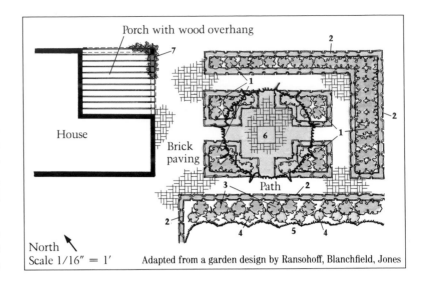

Adapted from a garden design by Ransohoff, Blanchfield, Jones

myrtle, lavender, santolina, yaupon holly, and azalea are also suitable plants.

A true parterre feels appropriate only with formal architecture and grounds. However, using hedges to define beds or walkways—a less formal treatment than a true parterre—is appropriate with New England, bungalow, and Victorian architecture.

A plane—land that is flat, sloped, or tipped but not undulating—is essential if geometric compositions are to look correct. If these shapes are placed on undulating or irregular land, the symmetry will look awkward. On anything steeper than a gently tipped plane, you will need to terrace the land or grade it into an even slope to make a parterre look natural.

1. Medium perennial (*Rosa* hybrid)
2. Low formal hedge (*Buxus microphylla* var. *japonica*)
3. Tall perennial (*Digitalis purpurea*)
4. Tall perennial (*Woodwardia radicans*)
5. Tall shrub (*Camellia japonica*)
6. Small pyramidal tree (*Citrus* 'Valencia')
7. Flowering vine (*Wisteria sinensis*)

## TREES

Gardens and trees are almost inseparable. Trees can provide shade, a canopy of spring flowers, and fall color. They can define a space and add sculptural qualities to a garden. They can cool the house in summer and let in winter sun. They can produce fruit. And they can provide a place for children to climb and to build a tree house.

Whatever their role, trees are one of the most significant elements in the garden because they are venerable and lend a sense of permanence. Think of the most attractive, established neighborhood in the community, and chances are it has tree-lined streets with gracious homes set off by mature trees.

When you are choosing a tree, consider the function it must perform and the visual quality it should provide. Do you need a shade tree to shelter the house and patio in summer, or do you need a flowering tree to serve as the focus of a garden view? Select trees with care; a thoughtfully chosen tree will provide years of pleasure.

## A Tree as Sculpture

The dramatic form or branching structure of a tree can lend an exciting, sculptural quality to the landscape. To show off such a tree, place it by itself in a prominent position in the garden. Keep in mind that space is a significant element of good design. The striking form of a tree is most noticeable if nothing is near it that distracts the eye.

Oak, camphor, beech, willow, and Camperdown elm are excellent sculptural trees. In this example the almost bizarrely twisted limbs of a camphor illustrate the striking effect of a sculptural tree, which can be heightened by providing a simple setting for it, as shown here. The lawn and low brick wall are monochromatic planes that provide clean, straight lines at the base of the tree. The contrast between the irregularity of the tree and those straight lines and monochromatic planes enhances the sculptural quality of the tree.

Trees with a sculptural form are usually slow growing, and designing a garden space around an element whose qualities may not be evident for 50 years can be frustrating. If there is not a mature tree on the property, consult a nursery, arboretum, or botanical garden to find out what sculptural trees are

relatively fast growing in your area. Don't overlook small fast-growing trees such as Japanese maple, which may be just right in a small city landscape.

A sculptural tree has a place in every style of garden. It fits quite naturally into a wild or informal garden, and it provides a lively contrast in a formal garden. Consider placing one sculptural tree at the end of a view, or frame a view by placing two trees close to the house on either side of a window. Keep in mind that a simple design treatment around the tree will set it off most effectively. So seek out your favorite tree; the opportunities to create a dramatic effect are considerable.

## An Allée

Single trees can be striking, but trees can also be grouped to define or strengthen an element in the landscape. In this classical tree-lined drive, rows of flowering plum trees emphasize the form of the driveway and also make it an attractive feature in the landscape. The rows of trees are called *allées*.

This composition contains only three elements: the driveway, the trees, and the hills in the background. The success of the composition is in its simplicity. Nothing distracts the eye—a significant factor when the space is designed to be moved through rather than stopped in. The design could be further strengthened by a row of mounding shrubs along each side of the driveway, which would emphasize the linear edge and prevent the eye from glancing out under the trees.

Allées can also define garden edges, create outdoor rooms in the garden, frame views, and emphasize land forms. Although allées are appropriate in both urban and rural settings, they are fairly formal. Yet they are compatible with any architecture except a rustic cabin. Keep in mind that rows, lines, and especially grids of trees look best on level land or evenly graded land; they will lose their impact on irregular land forms.

The time that trees take to achieve their maximum size depends on the species. In most cases fast-growing trees are short-lived. Check a local nursery for the trees that will be most appropriate for your situation.

## Trees for Seasonal Color

One of the most cherished qualities of a garden is its seasonal display of color. Flowering trees and trees exhibiting fall color provide this visual delight year after year. Most often planted solely for their flamboyant display of color, albeit of short duration, these trees are usually seen as individual specimens, although they are also effective when planted in groves or rows.

The memories and associations evoked by trees in seasonal color make them powerful elements in a landscape. Wherever such a tree is placed, it will act as a focal point. Whether it is a saucer magnolia in early spring, a jacaranda in midsummer, or a crape myrtle in early fall, a flowering tree will transform the space it occupies. The blaze of autumn color is every bit as dramatic as the flowers, from the deep red foliage of dogwood to the red-orange leaves of sugar maple and the yellow leaves of ash. In the examples shown here, dogwood proclaims the arrival of spring, casting a lacy veil over the landscape, and ginkgo scatters its striking yellow autumn leaves over the lawn and boxwood hedge.

The color of the blooms on a flowering tree should fit in with the color scheme of the garden. It can either harmonize or contrast with the dominant colors, as desired. The shape of the tree should also be in keeping with the style of the garden. Open, irregular trees, such as the dogwood and ginkgo in these examples, lend themselves well to naturally styled gardens and woodlands and also to more formal settings, where they may be used for intentional contrast. A formal tree with a fuller, more symmetrical shape, such as a Bradford pear, will enhance the sense of formality in a formal setting but may not harmonize well in a natural setting. For suggestions of variously shaped flowering trees that will do well in your garden, look for trees followed by the designation (F) under the appropriate climate zone in the "Landscape Plant Guide" starting on page 87.

Before you make a final choice, consider the appearance of the tree when it is not in flower or fall foliage, especially if you want to use it as a focal point. Its structure and habit must be worthy of its prominent position in the garden. Also consider from where the tree will be viewed while it is in bloom. Dogwood, with its upward-facing blooms, is best viewed from above, whereas Japanese snowdrop, with its drooping flowers, is best viewed from below. Don't forget that although they are sometimes considered a maintenance nuisance, fallen blossoms and leaves can have a lovely, if ephemeral, effect.

# GROUND COVERS

Relatively low-growing plants that are used to set off other garden features rather than to draw attention to the planting itself are referred to as ground covers. They provide a pleasing effect, control erosion on steep slopes, and form a green carpet on slopes where maintaining turf is impractical.

There are two groups of ground covers: trailing plants that root as they creep, forming a mass of uniform height; and low shrubs that have a naturally wide-spreading habit, which produces an undulating, mounded appearance. Grass is a type of ground cover, but the uniqueness of a lawn makes it worth individual attention (see page 49). In most cases ground covers require considerably less care than lawns; however, they usually take more time to fill in and cover an area.

To select a ground cover, study the plants' characteristics, including size, texture, color, flowers, and fruit. Some ground covers can be underplanted with bulbs for a seasonal burst of color. A ground cover that is thoughtfully selected and well cared for will suit any architectural style and will enhance almost any garden scheme.

## A Shaded Walk

The fine-textured, almost mossy ground cover in this side garden makes the narrow space feel cool and lush. The significant qualities of this ground cover are its very low habit and refined character. Its use in such an intimate setting promotes the feeling of seclusion that one might experience in a mossy glade in the woods. The paving stones provide contrast to the soft carpet of ground cover and highlight its creeping habit.

The tall shrubs and the high walls of the surrounding houses create seclusion in this urban setting. The shade is appealing here, but it is not necessary for all ground covers. Although most need moist, rich, well-drained soil to produce a lush effect, some ground covers, such as the creeping thymes, fare well in dry, sunny conditions.

Ground covers that are allowed to creep over retaining walls or paving stones, as shown here, produce a look of softness and permanence. Pleasing effects can be created by contrasting the refined texture of a ground cover with the broader, lusher foliage of adjacent perennials or shrubs.

This type of low-growing, fine-textured ground cover requires relatively little care—mainly just weeding while the ground cover is filling in. The need for weeding can be almost eliminated, however, by planting the ground cover into 3 to 4 inches of mulch or by applying a preemergent herbicide. Some ground covers benefit from periodic grooming and shearing, which is usually done after the plants have bloomed.

1. Small shade tree (*Acer palmatum*)
2. Medium pyramidal tree (*Prunus serrulata* 'Kwanzan')
3. Medium shrub (*Acer palmatum* 'Dissectum')
4. Low shrub (*Acer palmatum* 'Ever Red')
5. Medium shrub (*Camellia sasanqua* 'Showa-no-sakae')
6. Tall shrub (*Camellia japonica*)
7. Tall shrub (*Syzygium paniculatum*)
8. Low shrub (*Picea abies* 'Maxwellii')
9. Low shrub (*Chamaecyparis lawsoniana* 'Minima Aurea')
10. Low shrub (*Picea glauca* 'Conica')
11. Low shrub (*Picea abies* 'Pygmaea')
12. Medium shrub (*Rhododendron* 'Southern Charm')
13. Low shrub (*Rhododendron* 'Cilipinense')
14. Tall perennial (*Iris ensata*)
15. Low perennial (*Ophiopogon planiscapus* 'Nigrescens')
16. Low ground cover (*Laurentia fluviatilis*)
17. Medium ground cover (*Polystichum munitum*)
18. Low ground cover (*Ajuga reptans*)

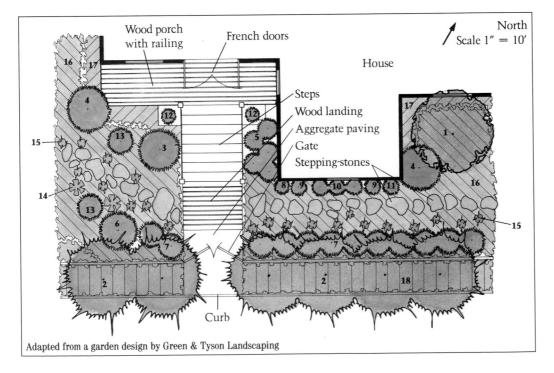

Adapted from a garden design by Green & Tyson Landscaping

## A Sunny Slope

A steep slope, particularly a large one, can be an imposing element in a garden and a challenge to landscape. It is prone to erosion by rain and difficult to irrigate—water will run off it. The keys to success are appropriate plants and a thoughtful composition.

A slope as steep and exposed as this one needs a ground cover to reduce erosion. The wide-spreading low shrubs chosen for this slope broaden quickly to hold the soil in place; they harmonize visually with the surrounding hillside; and they adapt well to poor, sun-baked soil.

A ground cover that grows rapidly and requires little water is ideal for a steep slope. It should be lightweight, so that it doesn't add too much weight to the top layer of soil and cause it to slough down the hill. It should tolerate poor soil and exposure to sun and wind, and be twiggy to break up rainwater. It should also be aesthetically pleasing. In this example the billowing, mounded form of the ground cover lends visual interest to a large planting, and it is particularly attractive in a spot where the low sun accentuates its shape in long shadows. The ground cover blends well with the surrounding wild landscape and at the same time provides an effective foreground to the taller flowering shrubs planted on the upper part of the slope.

The success of this landscape is also due to the careful arrangement of the plants. What could have been a vast expanse of hillside has been broken up with shrubs. The shrub and ground cover formations mimic the arrangement of the shrubs and grasses on the surrounding hills. On informal sites, informal arrangements of ground covers and shrubs can be used to create or enhance views or block undesirable views.

This informal composition for a steep slope works equally well on a level lot in hilly surroundings. It also works well on a wooded site or against a wooded backdrop, although a shaded site requires shade-tolerant plants. A more formal composition, however, would look more appropriate on a rectangular city lot. The informal design shown here adapts best to informal architectural styles.

A tough, nonflowering ground cover such as this requires very little care, since there is no need to prune or divide the plants or to cut the spent blooms.

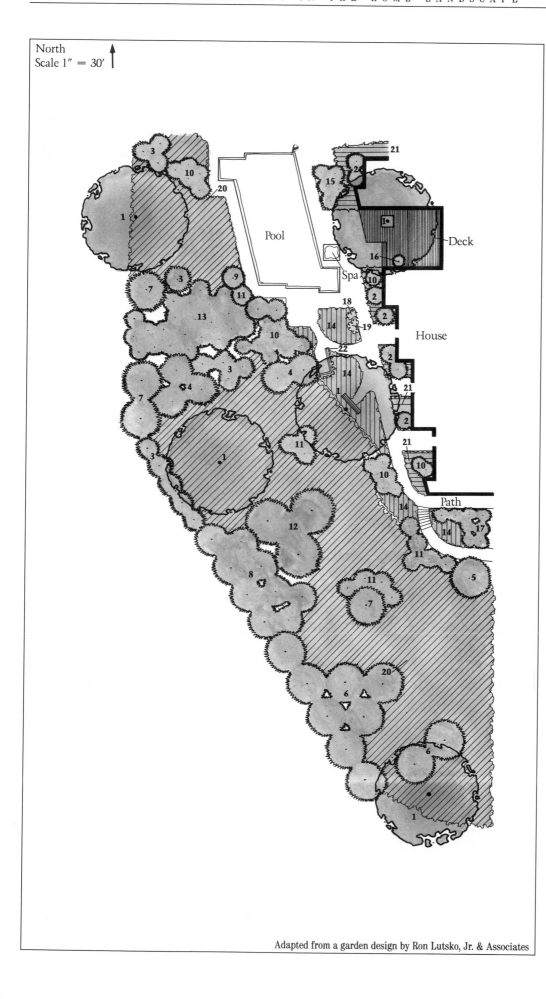

North
Scale 1″ = 30′

Adapted from a garden design by Ron Lutsko, Jr. & Associates

1. Large shade tree (*Quercus lobata*)
2. Tall shrub (*Arctostaphylos densiflora* 'Sentinel')
3. Tall shrub (*Arctostaphylos bakeri* 'Louis Edmunds')
4. Tall shrub (*Ceanothus* 'Concha')
5. Tall shrub (*Ceanothus* 'Ray Hartmann')
6. Tall shrub (*Cercocarpus betuloides*)
7. Tall shrub (*Fremontodendron* 'California Glory')
8. Tall shrub (*Heteromeles arbutifolia*)
9. Medium shrub (*Arctostaphylos* 'Sunset')
10. Medium shrub (*Arctostaphylos densiflora* 'Howard McMinn')
11. Low shrub (*Eriogonum arborescens*)
12. Medium shrub (*Ceanothus* 'Joyce Coulter')
13. Medium shrub (*Salvia clevelandii*)
14. Tall ground cover (*Arctostaphylos* 'Emerald Carpet')
15. Low shrub (*Arctostaphylos uva-ursi* 'Radiant')
16. Low shrub (*Mimulus aurantiacus*)
17. Low shrub (*Ribes viburnifolium*)
18. Low perennial (*Armeria maritima*)
19. Low perennial (*Eriogonum umbellatum*)
20. Tall ground cover (*Baccharis pilularis* 'Twin Peaks')
21. Tall ground cover (*Zauschneria californica*)
22. Flowering vine (*Clematis* sp.)

## A Forest Floor

Ground covers rambling among the perennials of the forest floor create an inviting image. The trees filter the light into dappled greens, producing a serene and cool effect, which is particularly pleasant during the warm months of summer. Here the arrangement of ground covers and ferns contributes to the restful, welcoming tone of such a landscape.

The randomly placed trees, with the branches cleared to at least eye level, establish the "forest." The modest diversity of ground covers and ferns makes the scene believable and helps tie it together. Keep in mind that a simple palette is preferable, with perhaps a few subtly colored flowering plants for accent if desired.

A meandering path sets off this scene and lets one wander through the cool woodland, taking in the feeling of peace. The path could be constructed of soil, mulch, leaves, stepping-stones, unit pavers, or gravel. A casual winding route, such as the one shown, is most appropriate; serpentine configurations should be avoided. A sense of enclosure completes the scene, disguising the apparent or real distance beyond and ensuring that the peaceful atmosphere is not disturbed by the surroundings.

To create a forest floor such as the one shown here, you will need existing mature trees or fast-growing new ones. If a few trees are already growing on the property, consider planting more trees of the same species to complete the sense of a forest. Select a ground cover of low-to-medium height; the "Landscape Plant Guide" starting on page 87 will help you choose plants that will do well in your climate zone. To accentuate the random planting of the trees, cluster perennials around the base of the trunks. Where trees form an ill-defined perimeter around a small space, add perennials to close the gaps in the perimeter and define the space. Think of subtle touches of seasonal color—spring growth, summer flowers, or autumn leaves—in soft or pale tones to lighten the shaded areas. If there are distracting elements in the background, retain the calm mood by enclosing the space with tall shrubs. Avoid hedges; they may look too formal in this setting.

North ←
Scale 1/16″ = 1′

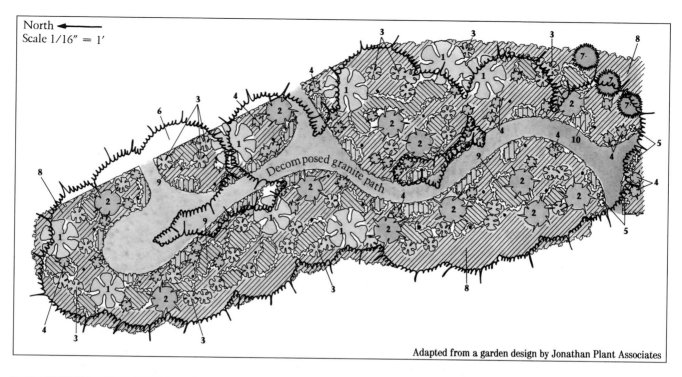

Decomposed granite path

Adapted from a garden design by Jonathan Plant Associates

*Asarum caudatum*

1. Tall perennial (*Dicksonia antarctica*)
2. Tall perennial (*Aralia californica*)
3. Tall perennial (*Woodwardia fimbriata*)
4. Medium perennial (*Polystichum munitum*)
5. Low perennial (*Cyclamen hederifolium*)
6. Large pyramidal tree (*Sequoia sempervirens*)
7. Medium shrub (*Rhododendron* hybrid)
8. Mixed medium ground cover (*Oxalis oregana, Asarum caudatum*)
9. Medium ground cover (*Vancouveria hexandra*)
10. Medium ground cover (*Galium odoratum*)

## FOUNDATION PLANTINGS

Originating with the traditional bungalow, foundation plantings were used to establish an intermediate level between the ground and the first floor of the house, which were often several feet apart. The plants not only visually linked the house to the ground, but they concealed the foundation and the basement windows. The decision whether to use foundation plantings depends on the architecture of the house. If you live in a simple, long, low structure designed to follow the horizontal lines of a desert setting, for example, foundation planting could obscure the relationship and negate the impact of the design.

Typically, foundation plantings form a skirt around a house. If they are well designed, they counterbalance the mass of the house, making it appear settled in the landscape. Foundation plantings can be designed as an extension of the architecture, as an extension of the landscape, or as the merging point of the two. To reflect the architecture of the house, foundation plantings should be arranged and clipped geometrically to emphasize the position of the doors, windows, walls, and niches. To reflect the landscape, they should be arranged irregularly and brought right to the foundation, where they will contrast with the geometry of the house. To merge the architecture and the landscape, foundation plantings should be arranged to follow the geometry of the house but allowed to reveal their natural form.

## Plantings of A Broken Rhythm

When a house with strong, contemporary architectural lines is placed in natural surroundings, a choice must be made whether to integrate the two. There are innumerable options, ranging from a strong contrast of the opposing forms to a subtle blending of them. This foundation planting merges the strong architectural lines with the landscape subtly but effectively.

The key elements in this design are the plants and the exterior alcoves of the house. The alcoves set up a broken rhythm of forms; that is, they suggest a pattern, but they are not set at precisely regular intervals.

The merging of the architectural lines with the landscape comes from the way the plants are placed and shaped. They are arranged in front of the walls in the same broken rhythm as the alcoves, so that they seem to be an extension of the architecture, yet have irregular, sculptural forms that resemble the natural forms of the surroundings. In this way they are connected both to the architecture of the house and to the wild landscape. Although these may seem lengthy reasons for a simple design, they explain why this planting feels comfortable and appropriate.

This composition of foundation planting adapts best to informal architectural styles; however, it may work with a formal house if the plants are placed in an even rhythm rather than a broken rhythm.

*Arctostaphylos densiflora* 'Howard McMinn'

1. Large shade tree (*Quercus lobata*)
2. Tall shrub (*Arctostaphylos densiflora* 'Sentinel')
3. Tall shrub (*Ceanothus* 'Concha')
4. Medium shrub (*Arctostaphylos densiflora* 'Howard McMinn')
5. Tall ground cover (*Arctostaphylos* 'Emerald Carpet')
6. Low shrub (*Arctostaphylos uva-ursi* 'Radiant')
7. Low shrub (*Mimulus aurantiacus*)
8. Low perennial (*Armeria maritima*)
9. Low perennial (*Eriogonum umbellatum* var. *polyanthum*)
10. Tall ground cover (*Baccharis pilularis* 'Twin Peaks')
11. Tall ground cover (*Zauschneria californica*)
12. Tall shrub (*Arctostaphylos bakeri* 'Louis Edmunds')
13. Medium shrub (*Salvia clevelandii*)
14. Medium shrub (*Arctostaphylos* 'Sunset')
15. Low shrub (*Eriogonum arborescens*)
16. Flowering vine (*Clematis* sp.)
17. Low shrub (*Ribes viburnifolium*)
18. Medium shrub (*Ceanothus* 'Joyce Coulter')

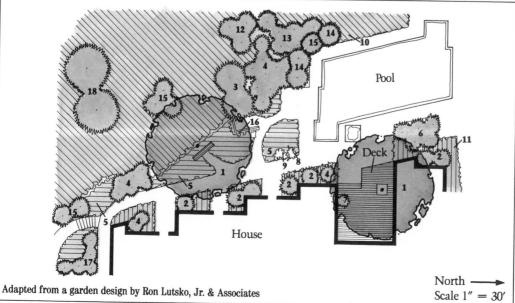

Adapted from a garden design by Ron Lutsko, Jr. & Associates

North →
Scale 1″ = 30′

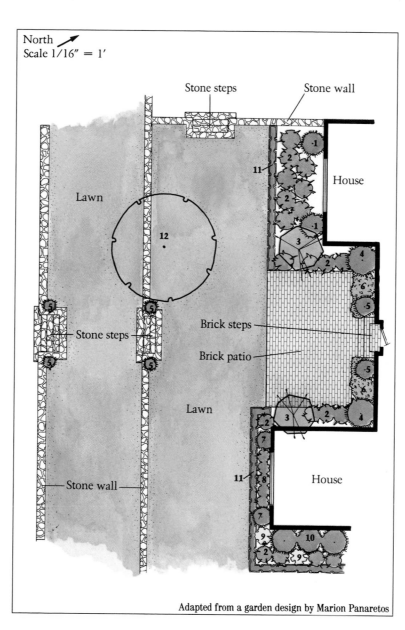

North
Scale 1/16″ = 1′

Stone steps    Stone wall

Lawn

House

12

Stone steps

Brick steps

Brick patio

Lawn

House

Stone wall

Adapted from a garden design by Marion Panaretos

1. Tall shrub (*Thuja occidentalis* 'Fastigiata')
2. Tall perennial (*Agapanthus orientalis*)
3. Medium broad-spreading tree (*Maytenus boaria*)
4. Medium shrub (*Acer palmatum* 'Dissectum')
5. Medium shrub (*Ligustrum japonicum*, potted)
6. Annuals (variety)
7. Tall shrub (*Chamaecyparis lawsoniana*)
8. Tall perennial (*Agapanthus africanus*)
9. Medium perennial (*Senecio* × *hybridus*)
10. Medium shrub (*Hydrangea macrophylla*)
11. Low formal hedge (*Buxus microphylla* var. *japonica*)
12. Medium narrow upright tree (*Betula pendula*)

## Architectural Plantings

One approach to designing foundation plantings is to use them to reflect the architecture of the house. In this example foundation plantings echo the house both in their formality and in the way their location and shapes accentuate the walls, windows, and doors.

The regularly placed plants emphasize and complement the strong, simple lines of the house. Light and views have been preserved by using low horizontal planting beds under the windows. The tall plants against the tall walls and the low plants under the windows extend the architectural forms of the house out into the garden.

The clipped hedges and the topiary in the planters accent the formality of the house, whereas the contrasting, colorful, and natural shapes of the perennials and flowering shrubs provide points of interest. The sense of formality might be heightened by using the informal shapes only for emphasis, to mark each side of the doorway, the corners of the house, or a significant window.

You can carry any architectural style into the garden with the proper foundation plantings. The architecture of the house should influence your choice of plants and the way you arrange them. Use the plantings to emphasize the architectural elements of the house and to reflect its formality or informality. Clipped hedges and topiary fit in well with formal architecture. Keep in mind, however, that the more formal the effect, the more care that will be required to keep the clipped topiary, hedges, and shrubs looking well manicured.

## PERENNIAL BORDERS

Few groups of plants provide as much color as perennials over such a long season and few can adapt to such a variety of conditions. For sheer diversity and richness, a well-planned perennial border is hard to beat.

True perennials are herbaceous plants that go dormant, usually in winter, but grow back year after year. With age they increase in size and produce more flowers. They also increase in number, providing new plants for colonizing other areas of the garden or sharing with friends. Most of the traditional favorites need rich, deeply worked soil and a great deal of water, but many perennials do well in a wide range of growing conditions—sites that are wet or dry, sunny or shaded, and soils that are rich or poor, deep or shallow, acid or alkaline. When you are choosing perennials for your garden, pay particular attention to what grows well in your area and to the water needs of the plants. In dry areas, drought-tolerant plants are the easiest to grow.

The diversity of perennials is one reason for their popularity. Thousands of varieties offer a range of flower color, period of bloom, and leaf shape, form, and texture that meets almost every need. Where winters are warm and gardens are expected to be in bloom the year around, perennial borders often include evergreen herbaceous flowering shrubs. They may also include many tender plants for color and exclude plants such as peonies that require winter chilling to perform well. The challenge in warm regions is to intermingle perennials and evergreen herbaceous plants for a pleasing year-round effect.

Regardless of where your garden is, expect your perennial border to need a lot of care. The diversity of the plants, the intensive use of the space, and the prolific flower production mean that you will spend many hours staking, pruning, grooming, watering, and fertilizing the plants, as well as removing dead flowers. Yet the continued popularity of perennials indicates that the maintenance is a fair trade for a pleasant hobby and many seasons of delight.

## A Woodland Border

Colorful plantings can be striking in the shade of mature trees. Here color livens up a pathway and accents the surrounding woods.

The success of this perennial garden is due to the existing mature trees and to the way the border plantings relate to the woodland. Plants that have woodland characteristics—ferns, large-leaved perennials, and rambling ground covers—harmonize the garden with the woodland understory. The natural arrangement of the path and the borders flanking it encourage the eye to follow the curve of the path through the sunlight-dappled woods. Light-colored foliage and flowers provide a contrast to the shade under the trees, and the controlled, repeated colors enhance the peaceful mood of this woodland walk.

A woodland garden can be established on almost any wooded site, or with the careful addition of trees, even in the shade of a tall building. Gently undulating sites, as seen

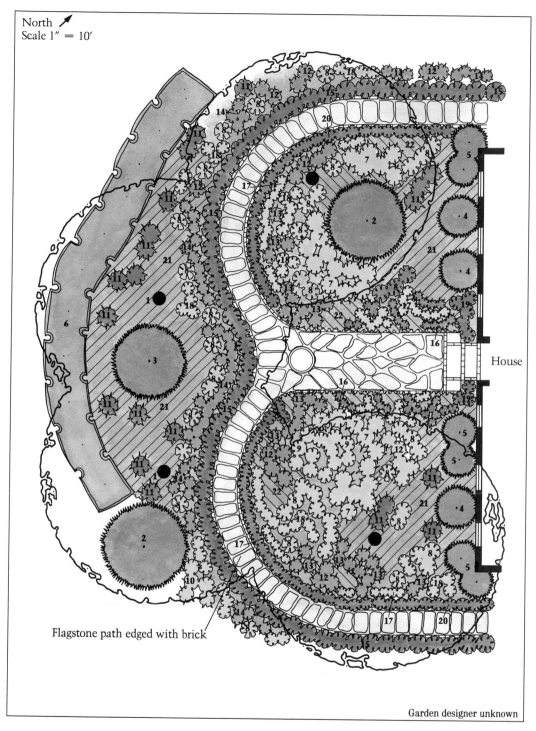

North
Scale 1" = 10'

Flagstone path edged with brick

House

Garden designer unknown

1. Large shade tree (*Quercus rubra*)
2. Tall shrub (*Hamamelis × intermedia*)
3. Tall shrub (*Viburnum plicatum* var. *tomentosum*)
4. Medium shrub (*Pieris japonica*)
5. Medium shrub (*Rhododendron keiskei*)
6. Medium formal hedge (*Fagus sylvatica* 'Atropunicea')
7. Tall perennial (*Hemerocallis* hybrid)
8. Tall perennial (*Hosta* hybrid)
9. Tall perennial (*Ligularia dentata*)
10. Tall perennial (*Lobelia cardinalis*)
11. Tall perennial (*Matteuccia pensylvanica*)
12. Medium perennial (*Dicentra eximia*)
13. Medium perennial (*Doronicum cordatum*)
14. Medium perennial (*Endymion non-scriptus*)
15. Medium perennial (*Hosta undulata*)
16. Medium perennial (*Mertensia virginica*)
17. Medium perennial (*Narcissus* hybrid)
18. Medium perennial (*Phlox divaricata*)
19. Medium perennial (*Trollius europaeus*)
20. Low perennial (*Primula × polyantha*)
21. Tall ground cover (*Polygonatum odoratum* 'Variegatum')
22. Medium ground cover (*Viola odorata*)

here, are ideal for their general aesthetic quality, but both level and sloping sites are satisfactory. A natural backdrop, where the garden looks as if it fades into the surrounding woods, is best, although an enclosing mass of shrubs or even vine-covered walls can work well. You can enhance the impression of lushness by contrasting large-leaved plants with small-leaved plants. Keep in mind, however, that large-leaved plants will dominate and can make a space appear smaller than it is.

This style of garden is usually associated with cottages and rustic shingled or wood-sided homes. It is also compatible with contemporary architecture. A woodland garden would be best located some distance from a large, stately house, with a more formal garden next to the building.

Very little maintenance is required for a garden of this design; more care is needed as you move from a natural look to a more refined look.

## A Traditional Border

The traditional English herbaceous border will always have a place in the heart of anyone who loves gardens. Typically bordering a walkway (hence the term *border*) and backed by a wall or tall shrubs, the long beds of perennials offer color throughout at least three seasons. The example shown here beautifully portrays the formal border style as it has been seen in England for more than a century.

Perennial borders most often have controlled color schemes, with either cool colors or warm colors predominating. In this example there are both cool pinks and purples and dominant warm yellows; the white flowers and silver and gray foliage blend them together. Keep in mind that you can change the dominating colors from season to season. Gertrude Jekyll, one of the best-known pioneers of this garden style, chose cool pinks and mauves and pastel yellows in the spring; stronger yellows, oranges, and reds at the height of summer; and the dusky blues and lavenders of her beloved Michaelmas daisies in the fall.

Color effects are strengthened if the colors are repeated throughout the border—using either more groups of the same perennial or groups of different perennials that echo the colors. The example demonstrates this clearly; repeating clumps of color lead the eye through the length of the border.

A classic herbaceous border relies mainly on perennials that are dormant in winter; however, in warm climates where a border can provide year-round display, evergreen herbaceous plants, whose shapes remain in all seasons, should be considered in order to maintain the garden's spatial character and form.

A traditional border such as the one shown here is most effective on relatively level, not undulating, terrain. A sunny location will allow you the greatest choice of plants, although a shaded perennial border can also be striking. Borders need a suitable background. In this example, the dark green foliage of the massed shrubs shows off the colorful plants; wood fencing and brick or stone walls also work well.

The layout of many traditional borders employs bilateral symmetry; on either side of the path the border has about the same depth and height, and the colors are picked up although not exactly matched. This symmetry lends an air of formality that complements formal or traditional architecture. A symmetrical arrangement is not essential to an herbaceous border, however; an asymmetric configuration is quite appropriate with informal and contemporary architecture.

1. Small shade tree (*Malus* hybrid)
2. Small broad-spreading tree (*Citrus* hybrid)
3. Tall shrub (*Escallonia rubra*)
4. Tall shrub (*Leptospermum scoparium*)
5. Tall shrub (*Philadelphus coronarius*)
6. Tall shrub (*Punica granatum*)
7. Medium shrub (*Artemisia* 'Powis Castle')
8. Medium shrub (*Caryopteris* × *clandonensis*)
9. Medium shrub (*Mahonia aquifolium*)
10. Medium shrub (*Philadelphus* × *lemoinei*)
11. Low shrub (*Santolina chamaecyparissus*)
12. Tall perennial (*Achillea filipendulina* 'Coronation Gold')

13. Tall perennial (*Chrysanthemum × superbum*)
14. Tall perennial (*Verbascum chaixii*)
15. Tall perennial (*Coreopsis verticillata*)
16. Tall perennial (*Dahlia* hybrid)
17. Tall perennial (*Echium fastuosum*)
18. Tall perennial (*Hemerocallis* hybrid)
19. Tall perennial (*Lychnis coronaria* 'Alba')
20. Tall perennial (*Oenothera tetragona*)
21. Tall perennial (*Penstemon* 'Midnight')
22. Tall perennial (*Salvia leucantha*)
23. Medium perennial (*Achillea × 'Moonshine'*)
24. Medium perennial (*Pelargonium peltatum*)
25. Medium perennial (*Veronica longifolia*)
26. Low perennial (*Dianthus deltoides*)
27. Low perennial (*Stachys byzantina*)
28. Annual (*Diascia barberae*)
29. Annual (*Cosmos bipinnatus*)

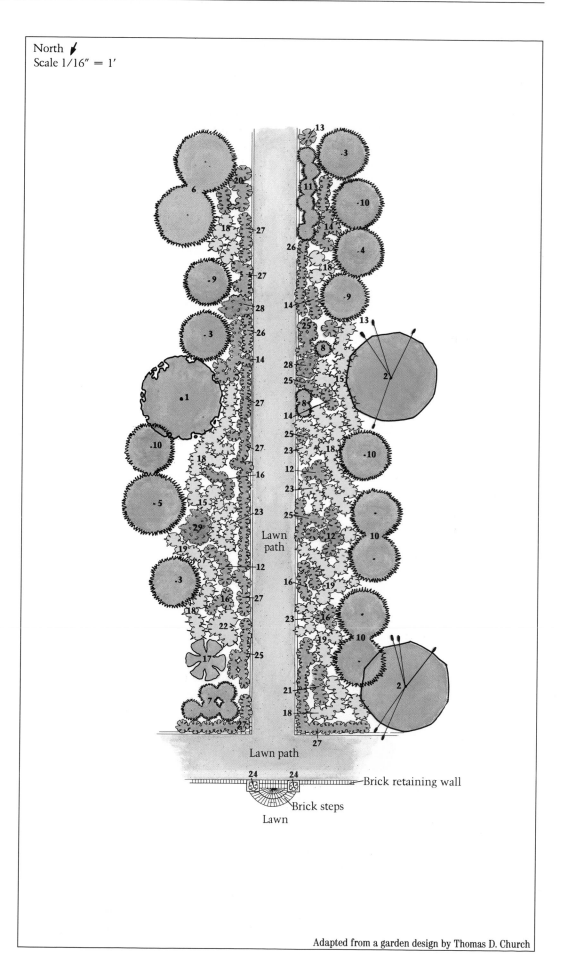

Adapted from a garden design by Thomas D. Church

# A Focal Border

This border of colorful perennials was placed to draw the attention of the viewer through the sloping property. The border's contrasting forms and continuous color throughout the seasons catch the eye and invite closer inspection. As visitors enter the garden at one end, they see the border at the farthest end. It arrests the eye by providing a point of focus—a place for the eye to stop and inspire the viewer to follow. Note on the landscape plan that the border itself is shown in detail; for simplicity, only general planting areas are indicated for the rest of the site.

The house sits at the highest point and extreme front edge of this property, a position that could well concentrate activity at the upper end, leaving the lower end unnoticed and unused. The border is designed to attract attention to the lower garden. It succeeds largely because of the color and form of the foliage and flowers and having the right setting to be noticed. The lawn is a restful space that contrasts with and shows off the rich diversity of the border.

The attention of the viewer is held by the balanced composition of the border. It is al-most formal in its balance: If the border were split in half, each half would be almost identical to the other. The symmetry is enhanced by the birdbath at the center of the border. The birdbath draws attention to the border, pinpointing its focus and terminating the view from the top of the slope. To help hold the viewer's attention and block undesirable views beyond, tall shrubs or evergreen trees could be planted behind the border.

Keep in mind that because a focal border is meant to attract attention and invite people to it, it should be placed in a spot that is accessible and welcoming. A perennial border can be created on virtually any site—sloped or flat, sunny or shaded. Choose plants that are hardy in your climate zone (see the "Landscape Plant Guide" starting on page 87) and that are compatible with your light and soil conditions.

A border with a wide variety of plants of different colors, shapes, and sizes suits all architectural styles except stark modern architecture, where the strikingly different qualities of the house and the border may not look comfortable together. For simple house styles, a border with less diversity of shape, color, and size is more appropriate.

1. Tall shrub
   (*Alyogyne huegelii*)
2. Medium shrub
   (*Artemisia* 'Powis Castle')
3. Low shrub
   (*Potentilla fruticosa* 'Abbotswood')
4. Tall perennial
   (*Aquilegia chrysantha*)
5. Tall perennial
   (*Artemisia absinthium* 'Lambrook Silver')
6. Tall perennial
   (*Lilium lancifolium*)
7. Tall perennial
   (*Penstemon* 'Holly's White')
8. Tall perennial
   (*Penstemon* 'Huntington Park')
9. Tall perennial
   (*Rudbeckia* 'Goldsturm')
10. Tall perennial
    (*Salvia pratensis*)
11. Tall perennial
    (*Salvia × superba* 'May Night')
12. Medium perennial
    (*Achillea ×* 'Moonshine')
13. Medium perennial
    (*Aquilegia* 'Snow Queen')
14. Medium perennial
    (*Aster ericoides*)
15. Medium perennial
    (*Gaillardia × grandiflora*)
16. Low perennial
    (*Heuchera sanguinea* 'Lillian's Pink')
17. Low perennial
    (*Erigeron ×* 'Moerheimii')
18. Low perennial
    (*Stachys byzantina* 'Silver Carpet')
19. Ornamental grass
    (*Helictotrichon sempervirens*)

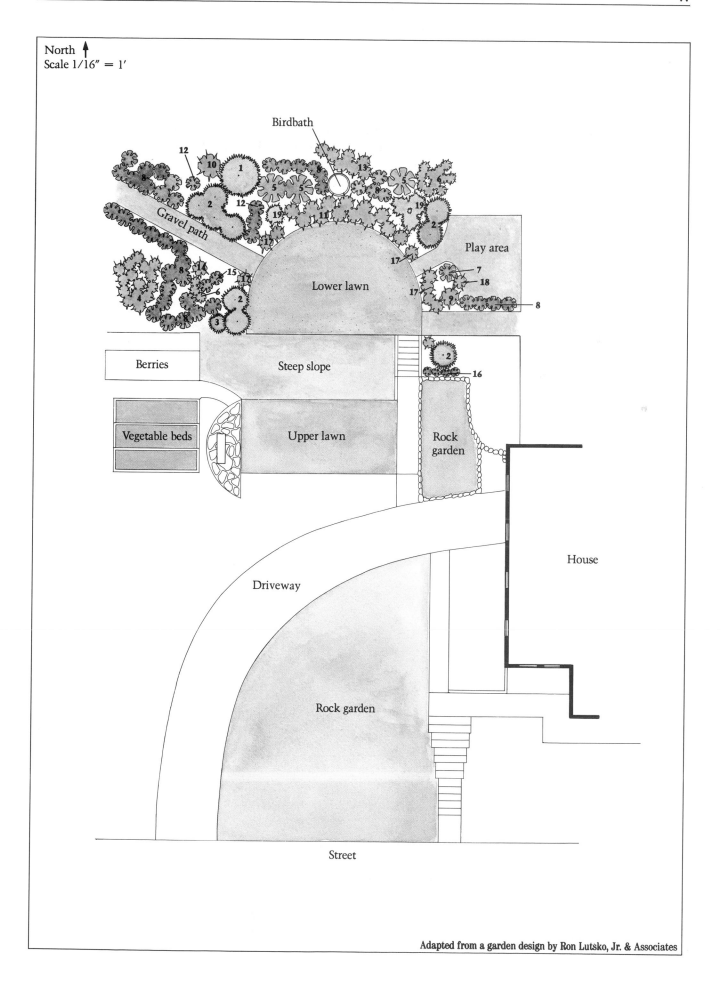

North
Scale 1/16″ = 1′

Birdbath

12
10
1
8
8
13
5
Gravel path
2
12
5
5
11
19
19
5
2
17
11
2
17
14
8
15
17
17
7
4
6
17
9
18
3
2
8
8

Play area

Lower lawn

Berries

Steep slope

2

Vegetable beds

Upper lawn

16

Rock garden

Rock garden

House

Driveway

Rock garden

Street

**Adapted from a garden design by Ron Lutsko, Jr. & Associates**

## A Sunny Border

The color and variation of a perennial border liven up a garden. In this example perennials embellish an otherwise austere palette; the green ground cover on the hillsides, the wide gray concrete walk, and the brown exterior walls of the house are relieved by the vibrance and diversity of the plantings.

The key to the success of this border is the way in which the plants both contrast with and yet fit the surroundings. Fit is determined by form, color, and texture. (To review the discussion of form, see page 9.) In this garden, fit is achieved with the mounding and spreading forms that simulate the hillside plantings, the subdued foliage color—few, if any, bright, shiny, or light greens—and the fine textures provided by small-leafed plants.

Since the area rimmed by this perennial border is the route to the entry and to the swimming pool, the plants are arranged to set up a rhythm that encourages movement. The plants lead you through the space rather than make you want to stop and look around. This rhythm is achieved by repeating certain plants along the border and by avoiding emphatic shapes that would lead your eye to the border and hold it there.

Herbaceous perennials, which compose most traditional borders, need a lot of care, including regular watering, trimming to the base, and dividing in fall or spring, according to the area. The border shown here, however, needs relatively little maintenance because it contains mostly evergreen perennials, many of which are drought tolerant. These plants do need full sun, though, and either good drainage or sparing amounts of water.

This border is most effective in surroundings that have visual characteristics similar to those of the border, in this example the mounding, spreading forms of the hillside plantings. If you place this border in front of a forest, the contrast between the border and the tall trees will be too great unless you use upright-growing plants with large leaves to harmonize with the lusher look of the forest.

A perennial border can be used to enliven the surroundings of formal or informal houses. It is effective in virtually any setting as long as the background is less diverse than the border and similar to it in form.

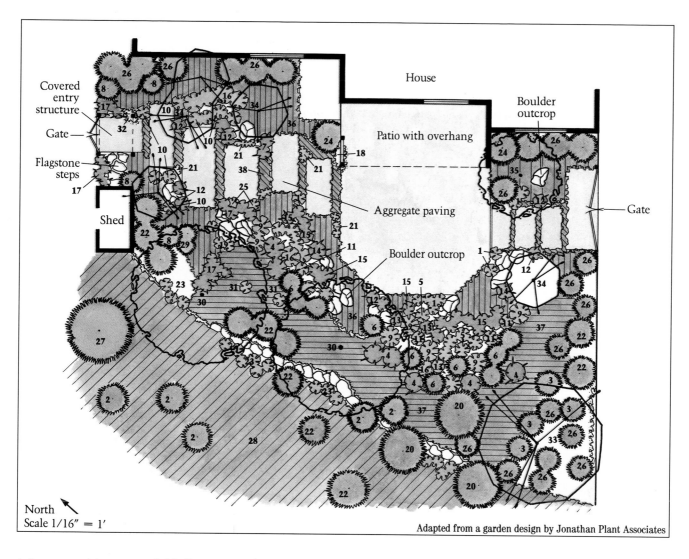

North
Scale 1/16" = 1'

Adapted from a garden design by Jonathan Plant Associates

1. Low perennial
(*Arenaria montana*)
2. Tall shrub
(*Arctostaphylos pajaroensis* 'Paradise')
3. Medium shrub
(*Arctostaphylos densiflora* 'Howard McMinn')
4. Medium perennial
(*Artemisia* 'Powis Castle')
5. Medium perennial
(*Caryopteris* × *clandonensis*)
6. Medium shrub
(*Cistus* × *skanbergii*)
7. Medium perennial
(*Diascia rigescens*)
8. Medium shrub
(*Carpenteria californica*)

9. Medium perennial
(*Chrysanthemum ptarmiciflorum* 'Silver Lace')
10. Low perennial
(*Eriogonum grande* var. *rubescens*)
11. Tall perennial
(*Gaura lindheimeri*)
12. Low perennial
(*Helichrysum argyrophyllum* 'Moe's Gold')
13. Tall perennial
(*Linaria purpurea*)
14. Tall perennial (*Iris* × *germanica*, white)
15. Medium perennial
(*Lavandula angustifolia* 'Hidcote')
16. Tall perennial
(*Penstemon* 'Midnight')

17. Medium perennial
(*Iris douglasiana*)
18. Flowering vine
(*Clematis montana* var. *rubens*)
19. Tall perennial
(*Gladiolus callianthus*)
20. Tall shrub
(*Melaleuca incana*)
21. Low perennial
(*Rhodohypoxis baurii* 'Letra Pink')
22. Medium shrub
(*Ceanothus* 'Julia Phelps')
23. Low perennial
(*Erigeron karvinskianus*)
24. Medium shrub
(*Prostanthera rotundifolia*)
25. Low perennial
(*Stachys byzantina*)

26. Medium shrub
(*Mahonia aquifolium*)
27. Tall shrub (*Myrica californica*)
28. Tall ground cover
(*Baccharis pilularis*)
29. Medium shrub
(*Salvia clevelandii*)
30. Large shade tree
(*Quercus rubra*)
31. Medium perennial
(*Convolvulus mauritanicus*)
32. Flowering vine
(*Hardenbergia violacea*)
33. Large broad-spreading tree
(*Quercus agrifolia*)
34. Small broad-spreading tree
(*Arbutus unedo*)
35. Small shade tree
(*Malus floribunda*)

36. Tall ground cover
(*Ceanothus griseus* var. *horizontalis*)
37. Medium ground cover
(*Arctostaphylos* 'Emerald Carpet')
38. Low ground cover
(*Herniaria glabra*)

## VEGETABLES AND HERBS

The visual delights of a food garden are as plentiful as the harvest. Whether you have space for a traditional vegetable garden or just a small kitchen herb garden, the forms, textures, and colors of culinary plants can enrich your landscape. Herbs can be treated formally—arranged geometrically and clipped meticulously in a traditional knot garden—or herbs and vegetables can be placed randomly between ornamental plants.

Among the virtues of a culinary garden is the provision of food that is fresh, flavorful, and nutritious. A food garden can be an exciting learning environment for children, giving them first-hand knowledge of simple botany and ecology. A culinary garden easily tended in raised beds can be a rewarding hobby for an elderly or a physically handicapped person.

Plant arrangement should be given the same emphasis in a food garden as it would receive in any other garden area. Vegetables and herbs can be integrated into the garden in such a way that they complement the other plants; or the food garden can be made a separate area, a special, even fun, place if the plants are arranged creatively.

### A Terraced Food Garden

The thoughtful arrangement of plants in this small raised-bed vegetable garden provides an attractive focus in the garden. Prominently located at the end of a small lawn, the garden expresses the owner's appreciation of the aesthetics of a well-maintained kitchen garden.

The stepped configuration of the raised beds results from the configuration of the site, which is sloped. Although terracing is obviously an apt choice for such a site, raised beds can be used almost anywhere for their visual interest and superior growing conditions. The soil of raised beds can be worked deeply; therefore, plants can be spaced much more closely than in a conventional garden and more food can be produced per square foot. This terraced food garden is only 12 feet wide by 11 feet long—each terrace is 4 feet wide by 11 feet long—yet during the harvest season

the garden produces more food than the family of four can eat.

A thoughtful arrangement of plantings can provide visual interest in a raised-bed garden. Contrasting colors can be played off one another—silver blue cabbage and broccoli; red-leaf lettuces, radicchio, and chard; and emerald green spinach. Onions, leeks, artichokes, and parsley can be added to provide effective contrast in form, and annuals can be added for more color. Herbs and ornamentals are used here to soften the edges of the raised beds and settle them into the landscape.

Various materials are suitable for raised beds, among them lumber, railroad ties, brick, cinder block, and stone. Be aware that some wood preservatives contain chemicals that should not be used near edible plants. Choose building materials that are compatible with materials used in the surroundings. For this site lumber was chosen and allowed to age to silver gray to match the wood-sided house, which is painted gray.

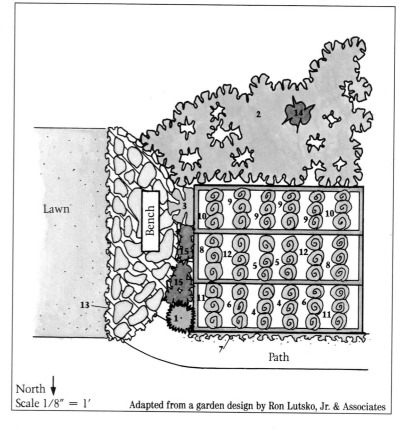

Lawn

Bench

Path

North ↓
Scale 1/8″ = 1′        Adapted from a garden design by Ron Lutsko, Jr. & Associates

*Lettuces and other greens*

1. Low shrub (*Lavandula angustifolia* 'Hidcote')
2. Medium perennial (*Penstemon heterophyllus*)
3. Low perennial (*Salvia officinalis* 'Purpurea')
4. Edible (black-seeded Simpson leaf lettuce)
5. Edible (garlic)
6. Edible (onions)
7. Edible (peas)
8. Edible (radicchio)
9. Edible (red chard)
10. Edible (red romaine lettuce)
11. Edible (red-leaf lettuce)
12. Edible (Swiss chard)
13. Medium ground cover (*Erigeron* × 'Moerheimii')
14. Tall perennial (*Iris* sp.)
15. Low perennial (*Heuchera sanguinea* 'Lillian's Pink')

## An Ornamental Food Garden

Vegetables do not need to be relegated to a separate space in the garden. Many have delightful forms, colors, and textures that can be visually pleasing in a border. Mixed plantings of ornamental and edible plants are practical in a garden too small for separate areas.

The pleasing and simple ornamental edible garden shown here is composed of elements often found in the home landscape—a lawn, a sitting area, borders, and screening plants. In this garden, however, areas that are traditionally planted with annuals, perennials, or low shrubs are planted with vegetables, with a touch of color from annuals to dress things up. (The brilliant marigolds have been planted to repel insects from other plantings in the area.)

The simplicity of the landscape is repeated in the vegetable border—a row of tomatoes in the background and basil in the foreground. The plants in the border should be chosen to suit the style of the rest of the garden and the culinary desires of the gardener.

Arrange culinary plants in much the same way as you would ornamental plants. Use the color of the foliage, flowers, and fruit to create either harmony or contrast. This is a good place to be bold and dramatic. Artichokes interplanted with red poppies make a striking picture; a combination of leeks, red-leaf lettuce, and forget-me-nots makes an attractive spring composition.

An ornamental edible garden—a delightful addition to any landscape—is especially

valuable in a small city garden with insufficient space for a vegetable garden and a traditional ornamental garden. In such a situation you might consider using edible plants in much the same way as annual bedding plants, flowering perennials, or small flowering shrubs—in pots and planters, in raised beds among decking or patio areas, as an edging for lawns and walks, and as a foreground for larger shrubs. Consider filling in other plantings with food crops; for instance, plant a border of parsley in front of a bed of bulbs, fill the bare spots left by dormant perennials with chard, or underplant roses with a variety of lettuces during the winter months. Start looking at vegetables in a new light to see the possibilities.

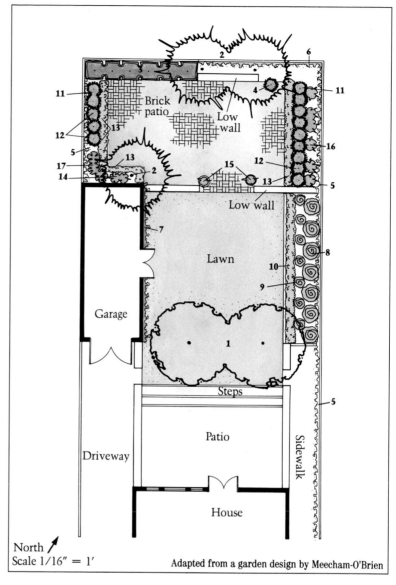

North
Scale 1/16″ = 1′

Adapted from a garden design by Meecham-O'Brien

1. Medium shade tree (*Fraxinus oxycarpa* 'Raywood')
2. Medium pyramidal tree (*Crataegus phaenopyrum*)
3. Medium formal hedge (*Ligustrum japonicum*)
4. Medium shrub (*Rhododendron* 'Red Poppy')
5. Flowering vine (*Jasminum polyanthum*)
6. Flowering vine (*Rosa banksiae*)
7. Flowering vine (*Wisteria sinensis*)
8. Edibles ('Early Girl' and 'Roma' tomatoes)
9. Edibles (*Ocimum basilicum*)
10. Annual (*Tagetes* 'Petite Yellow')
11. Low shrub (*Lavandula angustifolia*)
12. Low shrub (*Lavandula dentata*)
13. Annual (*Lobularia maritima*)
14. Medium perennial (*Brunnera macrophylla*)
15. Tall perennial (*Dietes bicolor*)
16. Tall perennial (*Iris* hybrid)
17. Tall perennial (*Iris ensata*)

## An Herb Garden

In addition to its culinary assets, an herb garden is a charming addition to a home landscape because of its rich textures and enticing fragrances. The blue-gray leaves of lavender, the purple leaves of some sages, and the golden-leafed form of oregano offer innumerable possibilities for interesting compositions.

Although many herbs are attractive enough to be included in a flower garden, they are often set off from the rest of the garden, as shown here, where tall plants at the periphery define and enclose the space. The thyme ground cover and the repetition of the lavender unify the composition of this herb garden. The tile paving and the bench are invitations to enter the space and to experience the delightful scent of thyme crushed underfoot. This herb garden occupies the corner of a suburban lot, but it enhances the surrounding landscape by exuding fragrance on warm afternoons and evenings.

An herb garden can be designed to harmonize with virtually any style of house. The classic, formal "knotted" herb garden with intertwining curved rows of low, compact plants fits in well with formal and traditional architecture. Herbs planted loosely or allowed to grow wild and look natural will suit simple and contemporary architecture. Herbs can be used in the landscape as flowering perennials or shrubs. Many species and cultivars of salvia, lavender, and rosemary are particularly well suited to this wider use.

Sunny, dry soil and good drainage are needed for most herbs; many thrive even in poor, gravelly conditions where few other plants can grow. Maintenance requirements vary according to the herbs you select. Thyme requires virtually no upkeep; neither does rosemary in warm climates. Chives need periodic dividing, and basil and parsley need to be replanted annually. Lavender needs to be cut back, but there is a bonus in that the clippings can be used ornamentally for their fragrance or flowers. Oregano also needs to be cut back, but the clippings are the harvest. If you do not use the herb clippings fresh in cooking, you can hang many herbs upside down to dry in a cool, dark place, then crush, sift, and store them in jars for future use.

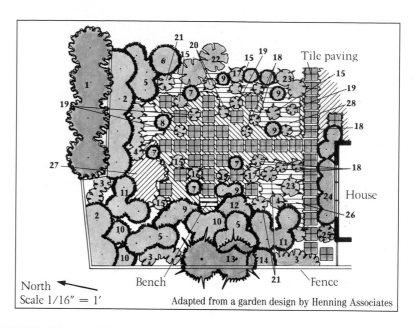

North
Scale 1/16″ = 1′

Adapted from a garden design by Henning Associates

1. Tall screen (*Prunus laurocerasus*)
2. Tall shrub (*Nerium oleander*)
3. Tall perennial (*Woodwardia* sp.)
4. Tall perennial (*Strelitzia reginae*)
5. Medium shrub (*Cistus × purpureus*)
6. Tall shrub (*Brunfelsia pauciflora* 'Floribunda')
7. Low shrub (*Santolina chamaecyparissus*)
8. Low shrub (*Santolina virens*)
9. Low shrub (*Lavandula angustifolia*)
10. Medium shrub (*Juniperus chinensis* 'Pfitzerana Blue-Gold')
11. Medium shrub (*Cistus × hybridus*)
12. Low shrub (*Lavandula dentata*)
13. Small pyramidal tree (*Citrus* 'Valencia', standard)
14. Medium shrub (*Hydrangea macrophylla*)
15. Low perennial (*Thymus × citriodorus*)
16. Tall perennial (*Mentha × piperita*)
17. Low perennial (*Salvia officinalis* 'Icterina')
18. Low perennial (*Stachys byzantina*)
19. Medium perennial (*Achillea millefolium* 'Fire King')
20. Medium perennial (*Thymus vulgaris*)
21. Tall perennial (*Pelargonium × domesticum*)
22. Tall perennial (*Echium fastuosum*)
23. Tall perennial (*Pelargonium × hortorum*)
24. Medium shrub (*Hebe* 'Coed')
25. Low perennial (*Viola odorata*)
26. Mixed low ground cover (*Thymus pseudolanuginosus, Chamaemelum nobile* 'Treneague')
27. Tall ground cover (*Rosmarinus officinalis* 'Prostratus')
28. Low ground cover (*Thymus praecox arcticus*)

# Landscape Plant Guide

*The best landscape plants for all climate zones are listed in this guide. Choose the plants that thrive in your area. Plants are keyed to the landscape plans in the preceding chapter.*

T o inspire your choice of plants for your landscape, this chapter contains suggestions for plants that should grow well in your climate zone. Plants for eight USDA climate zones in the continental United States are arranged in the same categories given in the landscape plans—shade trees, landscape trees, screens, informal hedges, formal hedges, shrubs, ground covers, perennials, ornamental grasses, and vines.

This chapter is meant as a starting point for your plant selection. A visit to a local nursery will uncover many other plants suitable for your area. Since climate conditions vary within each zone, plant performance also varies, so consult the nursery staff before making your final selection.

*This well-composed garden with plants of varied texture and color is a source of continuing delight for the garden designer and for visitors strolling along the path.*

## PLANT NAMES

Each plant in this chapter is listed by both its botanical name and its common name. Plant growers and retailers across the country use botanical names because common names vary. Usually consisting of two words, the genus and species, the botanical name ensures that you get the plant you asked for.

You will see that many of the plant names consist of more than the genus and species names. The additional words, usually set off by single quotes, name the cultivar; for example, *Magnolia grandiflora* 'St. Mary' is the St. Mary cultivar of southern magnolia. Short for "cultivated variety," a cultivar is a plant with a particular set of characteristics, selected from among individual plants in the species. To ensure that the desirable traits possessed by the cultivar—for example, showy flowers or variegated leaves—are retained in the new plants, cultivars are propagated from cuttings or grafts rather than from seed.

When you are using the lists in this chapter to select a plant for a particular use, be sure to note the cultivar names. There can be many cultivars of a given species, and their habits can be vastly different. For example, *Quercus robur* 'Fastigiata', the upright English oak, is a narrow, upright tree. Other members of the species grow from 75 to 150 feet tall with an open, broad head—hardly narrow and upright!

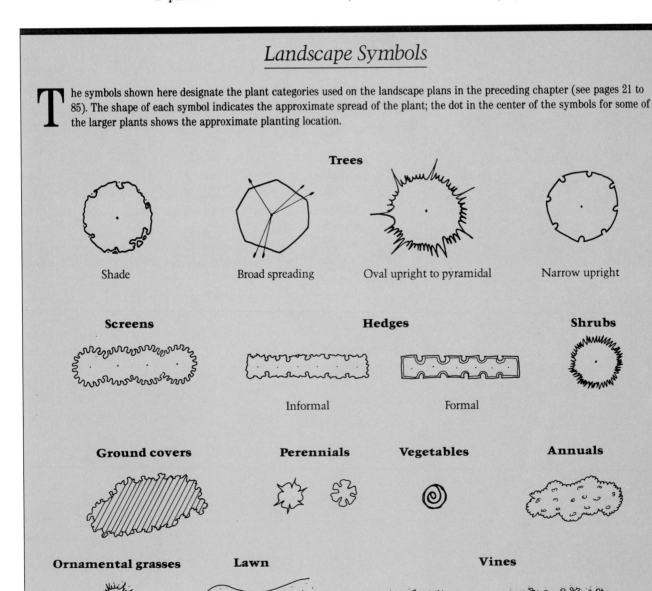

## Landscape Symbols

The symbols shown here designate the plant categories used on the landscape plans in the preceding chapter (see pages 21 to 85). The shape of each symbol indicates the approximate spread of the plant; the dot in the center of the symbols for some of the larger plants shows the approximate planting location.

**Trees**

Shade          Broad spreading          Oval upright to pyramidal          Narrow upright

**Screens**          **Hedges**          **Shrubs**

Informal          Formal

**Ground covers**          **Perennials**          **Vegetables**          **Annuals**

**Ornamental grasses**          **Lawn**          **Vines**

Nonflowering          Flowering

## CLIMATE ZONES

Locate your climate zone on the map below, which is based on the USDA map of climate zones. Then on the following pages find the plant list for your zone. You will notice that zones are grouped together (zones 3 and 4, 5 and 6, 7 and 8, and 9 and 10), and that some plants are followed by a number, which indicates that the plant is hardy in that zone but not the other. If no number is given, the plant is hardy in both zones. If you live in the extreme northern part of Minnesota (zone 2), consult the plant list for zone 3; the plants suggested for zone 3 are hardy in your area.

The map is intended as a guide to selecting plants that grow well in most situations in each area. Be aware, however, that the zone designations are based on average data. Your local climate may be warmer, especially if you live near the ocean, or it may be colder, especially in mountain regions. If you live at a higher elevation than the average for your state, your climate may be from one to three zones colder than shown on the map. If your garden is on a north-facing slope, it is one zone colder.

In addition to temperature, soil type may affect the suitability of a particular species to your garden. Rhododendrons, for example, prefer acid to alkaline soil and well-drained loam to heavy clay soil.

Keep these limitations in mind as you start to choose plants for your landscape.

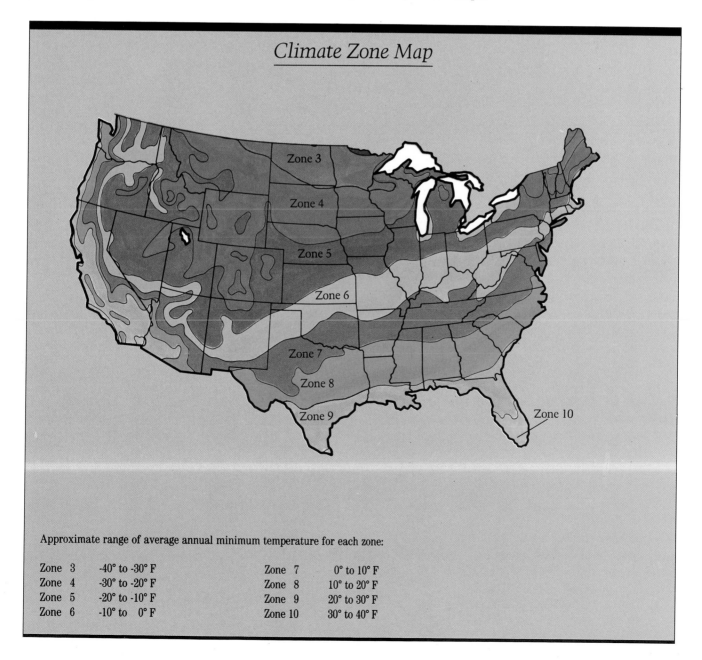

*Climate Zone Map*

Zone 3
Zone 4
Zone 5
Zone 6
Zone 7
Zone 8
Zone 9
Zone 10

Approximate range of average annual minimum temperature for each zone:

| Zone | 3 | -40° to -30° F | | Zone | 7 | 0° to 10° F |
| Zone | 4 | -30° to -20° F | | Zone | 8 | 10° to 20° F |
| Zone | 5 | -20° to -10° F | | Zone | 9 | 20° to 30° F |
| Zone | 6 | -10° to  0° F | | Zone | 10 | 30° to 40° F |

## PLANT GUIDE

The following plants will grow well in most situations in each climate zone for which they are listed (see Climate Zones, page 89). The type of soil in your garden and your exact location will affect the growth of some plants, however, so consult a local nursery to make sure your selection is appropriate.

If you live in an area where winters are warm and gardens are expected to be in bloom the year around, you will appreciate the designation (D) beside plants that either die back to the ground or lose their leaves in winter. Plants without this designation are conspicuously present in the garden the year around. The designation (F) beside individual plants indicates those that have showy flowers for at least part of the year.

The plants suggested as shade trees are deciduous in all zones. Those suggested as broad-spreading landscape trees—not typically thought of as shade trees—are evergreen in all zones except 3/4 and 5/6, where the cold winters suit only a few evergreens that merit attention.

Landscape trees listed in the categories for oval upright to pyramidal and narrow upright include both deciduous and evergreen trees for all zones. Except for zones 3/4 and 5/6, plants suggested as screens are dense evergreen trees or shrubs that provide excellent visual screening. (The deciduous screens are sufficiently twiggy that they are also effective for visual screening.)

When choosing shrubs and hedges, keep in mind that the plants suggested as shrubs perform well as single specimens or in small groups, whereas the plants suggested as hedges are well suited for defining a space. Plants suggested as formal hedges respond well to being sheared. Many of the plants suggested as shrubs and hedges can be used interchangeably. Consult a local nursery if you have questions about how to use a particular plant.

## ZONES 3 AND 4

### Shade Trees

#### Small (10–25 ft)

*Acer ginnala* (Amur maple) (D)
*Amelanchier laevis* (serviceberry, shadbush) (D) (F)
*Carpinus caroliniana* (American hornbeam) (D)
*Cornus alternifolia* (pagoda dogwood) (D)
*Prunus cerasifera* (cherry plum) (4) (D) (F)

#### Medium (25–40 ft)

*Acer negundo* (box elder, ash-leaved maple) (D)
*Betula populifolia* (gray birch, clump birch) (D)
*Ostrya virginiana* (hop hornbeam) (D)
*Sorbus aucuparia* (European mountain ash) (D) (F)
*Syringa reticulata* (Japanese tree lilac) (D) (F)

*Sorbus aucuparia* (European mountain ash)

**Large (more than 40 ft)**

*Acer rubrum* (red maple) (D)
*Acer saccharum* (sugar maple) (D)
*Fraxinus pennsylvanica*
(green ash) (D)
*Quercus rubra* (red oak) (D)
*Tilia cordata* (littleleaf
linden) (D)

## Landscape Trees

### BROAD SPREADING

**Small (10–25 ft)**

*Chionanthus virginicus*
(old-man's-beard) (4) (D) (F)
*Crataegus viridis* 'Winter King'
(winter king hawthorn) (4) (D) (F)
*Elaeagnus angustifolia*
(Russian olive) (D)
*Hamamelis virginiana* (common
witch hazel) (D) (F)
*Malus × atrosanguinea*
(carmine crabapple) (4) (D) (F)

**Medium (25–40 ft)**

*Aesculus glabra*
(Ohio buckeye) (D) (F)
*Amelanchier × grandiflora*
(serviceberry, shadbush) (D) (F)
*Carpinus caroliniana* (American
hornbeam) (D)
*Malus baccata* (Siberian
crabapple) (D) (F)
*Phellodendron amurense*
(Amur cork tree) (4) (D) (F)

**Large (more than 40 ft)**

*Celtis occidentalis* (hackberry) (D)
*Cladrastis lutea*
(yellowwood) (4) (D) (F)
*Fraxinus pennsylvanica* 'Marshall'
(Marshall seedless ash) (D)
*Gleditsia triacanthos*
(honey locust) (D)
*Salix pentandra* (laurel willow) (D)

### OVAL UPRIGHT TO PYRAMIDAL

**Small (10–25 ft)**

*Cotinus coggygria*
(smokebush) (4) (D) (F)
*Hydrangea paniculata* 'Grandiflora'
(peegee hydrangea) (D) (F)
*Malus* 'Pink Spires' (pink spires
crabapple) (4) (D) (F)
*Pinus mugo* (Swiss mountain pine)
*Viburnum lantana*
(wayfaring tree) (D) (F)

**Medium (25–40 ft)**

*Alnus glutinosa* (European
alder) (4) (D)
*Juniperus scopulorum*
(Rocky Mountain juniper)
*Picea omorika* (Serbian spruce)
*Sorbus alnifolia* (Korean
mountain ash) (4) (D) (F)
*Thuja occidentalis* (American
arborvitae)

*Cotinus coggygria* (smokebush)

*Picea pungens* (Colorado spruce)

## Large (more than 40 ft)

*Larix decidua* (European larch) (D)
*Picea pungens* (Colorado spruce)
*Pinus flexilis* (limber pine)
*Pseudotsuga menziesii*
   (Douglas fir) (4)
*Tsuga canadensis* (Canada hemlock)

## NARROW UPRIGHT

### Small (10–25 ft)

*Caragana arborescens* (Siberian
   pea tree) (D) (F)
*Juniperus chinensis* (Chinese
   juniper, upright varieties) (4)
*Malus* 'Sentinel' (sentinel
   crabapple) (4) (D) (F)
*Rhamnus frangula* 'Columnaris'
   (tallhedge alder buckthorn) (D)
*Sorbus aucuparia* 'Fastigiata'
   (fastigiate European mountain
   ash) (D) (F)

### Medium (25–40 ft)

*Carpinus betulus* 'Columnaris'
   (columnar European
   hornbeam) (4) (D)
*Juniperus virginiana* (red cedar)
*Malus baccata* 'Columnaris'
   (columnar Siberian
   crabapple) (D) (F)
*Pinus sylvestris* 'Fastigiata'
   (fastigiate Scots pine)
*Thuja occidentalis* (American
   arborvitae)

### Large (more than 40 ft)

*Acer platanoides* 'Columnare'
   (columnar Norway maple) (4) (D)
*Acer rubrum* 'Columnare'
   (columnar red maple) (D)
*Ginkgo biloba* 'Fastigiata' (fastigiate
   maidenhair tree) (4) (D)
*Pinus strobus* 'Fastigiata' (fastigiate
   eastern white pine)
*Quercus robur* 'Fastigiata' (fastigiate
   English oak) (4) (D)

## Screens

### Low (5–8 ft)

*Cornus alba* (Tatarian
   dogwood) (D) (F)

*Cornus racemosa*
   (gray dogwood) (D) (F)
*Euonymus alata* (winged
   euonymus) (D)
*Myrica pensylvanica*
   (bayberry) (4) (D)
*Rosa rugosa* (rugosa rose) (D) (F)

### Medium (8–15 ft)

*Ligustrum amurense*
   (Amur privet) (D) (F)
*Osmanthus × fortunei*
   (Fortunes osmanthus)
*Rhamnus frangula* 'Columnaris'
   (tallhedge alder buckthorn) (D)
*Syringa villosa* (late lilac) (D) (F)
*Viburnum prunifolium*
   (black haw) (4) (D) (F)

### Tall (more than 15 ft)

*Acer ginnala* (Amur maple) (D)
*Elaeagnus angustifolia*
   (Russian olive) (D)
*Pseudotsuga menziesii*
   (Douglas fir) (4)
*Thuja occidentalis* (American
   arborvitae)
*Tsuga canadensis* (Canada
   hemlock)

## Informal Hedges
(less than 5 ft)

*Berberis thunbergii* 'Kobold'
   (Kobold Japanese barberry) (4) (D)
*Juniperus chinensis* 'Armstrongii'
   (Armstrong juniper) (4)
*Potentilla fruticosa* (shrubby
   cinquefoil) (D) (F)
*Taxus cuspidata* 'Nana'
   (dwarf Japanese yew) (4)
*Viburnum opulus* 'Nanum'
   (dwarf European cranberry
   bush) (D) (F)

## Formal Hedges

### Low (less than 3 ft)

*Berberis thunbergii* 'Crimson Pygmy'
   (crimson pygmy Japanese
   barberry) (4) (D)
*Buxus microphylla* (littleleaf
   boxwood) (4)

*Physocarpus opulifolius* 'Nanus'
   (dwarf ninebark) (D) (F)
*Ribes alpinum* (alpine currant) (D)
*Salix purpurea* 'Nana' (dwarf
   purple osier) (D)

### Medium (3–6 ft)

*Berberis thunbergii*
   (Japanese barberry) (4) (D)
*Cotoneaster lucidus*
   (hedge cotoneaster) (D)
*Euonymus alata* (winged
   euonymus) (D)
*Ligustrum amurense*
   (Amur privet) (D) (F)
*Taxus cuspidata* (Japanese yew) (4)

### Tall (6–15 ft)

*Juniperus virginiana* (red cedar)
*Rhamnus frangula* 'Columnaris'
   (tallhedge alder buckthorn) (D)
*Thuja occidentalis* (American
   arborvitae)
*Tsuga canadensis* (Canada hemlock)
*Viburnum prunifolium* (black
   haw) (4) (D) (F)

## Shrubs

### Low (less than 3 ft)

*Hydrangea arborescens* 'Grandiflora'
   (snowhill hydrangea) (D) (F)
*Potentilla fruticosa* (shrubby
   cinquefoil) (D) (F)
*Spiraea × bumalda*
   (bumald spirea) (D) (F)
*Thuja occidentalis* (American
   arborvitae, dwarf types)
*Viburnum opulus* 'Nanum'
   (dwarf European
   cranberry bush) (D) (F)

### Medium (3–6 ft)

*Acanthopanax sieboldianus*
   (fiveleaf aralia) (D)
*Cornus alba* (Tatarian
   dogwood) (D) (F)
*Forsythia ovata* (Korean
   forsythia) (4) (D) (F)
*Myrica pensylvanica*
   (bayberry) (4) (D)
*Symphoricarpos rivularis*
   (snowberry) (D) (F)

## Tall (6–15 ft)

*Acer ginnala* (Amur maple) (D)
*Juniperus virginiana* (red cedar)
*Lonicera tatarica* (Tatarian
honeysuckle) (D)
*Syringa vulgaris*
(common lilac) (D) (F)
*Viburnum dentatum*
(arrowwood) (D) (F)

# Ground Covers

## Low (less than 4 in.)

*Ajuga reptans* (carpet bugle) (F)
*Euonymus fortunei* 'Minima'
(baby wintercreeper) (4)
*Juniperus horizontalis* 'Wiltonii'
(blue rug juniper)
*Sedum acre* (yellow stonecrop) (F)
*Thymus praecox arcticus*
(mother-of-thyme) (F)

## Medium (4–12 in.)

*Arctostaphylos uva-ursi*
(bearberry) (F)
*Convallaria majalis*
(lily-of-the-valley) (D) (F)
*Epimedium* (barrenwort) (D) (F)
*Juniperus horizontalis*
(creeping juniper, selected cultivars)
*Lamium maculatum* (spotted dead
nettle) (D) (F)

## Tall (12–30 in.)

*Diervilla lonicera* (dwarf bush
honeysuckle) (D)
*Juniperus sabina* (savin,
selected cultivars)
*Rhus aromatica* 'Gro-low' (fragrant
sumac) (4) (D)
*Symphoricarpos mollis* (Indian
currant) (D) (F)
*Vinca major* (greater
periwinkle) (4) (F)

# Perennials

## Low (less than 10 in.)

*Arabis caucasica*
(wall rock cress) (F)
*Campanula carpatica* (Carpathian
bellflower) (D) (F)
*Phlox subulata* (moss pink) (F)

*Paeonia lactiflora* (garden peony)

*Primula × polyantha* (polyanthus,
primrose) (D) (F)
*Veronica prostrata* (Hungarian
speedwell) (F)

## Medium (10–24 in.)

*Astilbe × arendsii* (astilbe) (D) (F)
*Chrysanthemum × morifolium*
(florist's chrysanthemum) (D) (F)
*Hemerocallis* (daylily, selected
cultivars) (D) (F)
*Hosta* (plantain lily) (D) (F)
*Paeonia lactiflora*
(garden peony) (D) (F)

## Tall (more than 24 in.)

*Aconitum carmichaelii*
(monkshood) (D) (F)
*Anemone × hybrida*
(Japanese anemone) (D) (F)
*Aster novae-angliae*
(New England aster) (D) (F)
*Cimicifuga racemosa* (black
snakeroot) (D) (F)
*Veronicastrum virginicum*
(culvers root) (D) (F)

# Ornamental Grasses

*Chasmanthium latifolium* (northern
sea oats, wild oats) (D)

*Festuca ovina* var. *glauca*
(blue fescue)
*Miscanthus sinensis* (eulalia grass,
selected cultivars) (D)
*Panicum virgatum* (switch grass) (D)
*Pennisetum alopecuroides*
(Chinese pennisetum) (D)

# Vines

*Ampelopsis brevipedunculata*
(porcelain vine) (4) (D)
*Aristolochia durior*
(Dutchman's-pipe) (4) (D)
*Campsis radicans* (trumpet
vine) (4) (D) (F)
*Celastrus scandens* (American
bittersweet) (D)
*Clematis dioscoreifolia* var. *robusta*
(sweet autumn clematis) (4) (D) (F)
*Clematis × jackmanii*
(Jackman clematis) (D) (F)
*Hedera helix* 'Baltica' (Baltic ivy)
*Parthenocissus quinquefolia*
(Virginia creeper) (D)
*Polygonum aubertii*
(silver lace vine) (4) (D) (F)
*Wisteria floribunda* (Japanese
wisteria) (4) (D) (F)

# ZONES 5 AND 6

## Shade Trees

### Small (10–25 ft)
*Acer ginnala* (Amur maple) (D)
*Acer palmatum* (Japanese maple) (D)
*Carpinus caroliniana* (American hornbeam) (D)
*Cornus alternifolia* (pagoda dogwood) (D)

### Medium (25–40 ft)
*Acer campestre* (hedge maple) (D)
*Celtis occidentalis* (hackberry) (D)
*Cercidiphyllum japonicum* (katsura tree) (D)
*Fraxinus oxycarpa* 'Raywood' (Raywood ash) (D)
*Zelkova serrata* (Japanese zelkova) (6) (D)

### Large (more than 40 ft)
*Acer saccharum* (sugar maple) (D)
*Cladrastris lutea* (yellowwood) (D) (F)
*Liquidambar styraciflua* (sweet gum) (6) (D)

*Quercus palustris* (pin oak) (D)
*Tilia cordata* (littleleaf linden) (D)

## Landscape Trees

### BROAD SPREADING

#### Small (25–40 ft)
*Cornus kousa* (Japanese dogwood) (D) (F)
*Juniperus chinensis* 'Glauca Hetzii' (Hetz blue juniper)
*Malus sargentii* (Sargent crabapple) (D) (F)
*Syringa reticulata* (Japanese tree lilac) (D) (F)
*Thuja occidentalis* 'Nigra' (dark green arborvitae)

#### Medium (25–40 ft)
*Carpinus caroliniana* (American hornbeam) (D)
*Cornus florida* (flowering dogwood) (D) (F)
*Halesia carolina* (Carolina silverbell) (D)
*Ilex crenata* (Japanese holly)
*Taxus baccata* 'Repandens' (spreading English yew)

### Large (more than 40 ft)
*Fraxinus americana* 'Autumn Applause' (autumn applause white ash) (D)
*Ilex opaca* (American holly)
*Pinus nigra* (Austrian pine)
*Quercus rubra* (red oak) (D)
*Taxus cuspidata* (Japanese yew)

### OVAL UPRIGHT TO PYRAMIDAL

#### Small (10–25 ft)
*Ilex crenata* 'Latifolia' (bigleaf holly) (6)
*Juniperus scopulorum* 'Gray Gleam' (gray gleam juniper)
*Malus* 'Indian Magic' (Indian magic crabapple) (D) (F)
*Malus* 'Pink Spires' (pink spires crabapple) (D) (F)
*Viburnum lantana* (wayfaring tree) (D) (F)

#### Medium (25–40 ft)
*Aesculus* × *carnea* (red horse chestnut) (D)
*Amelanchier canadensis* (shadbush serviceberry) (D)

*Cornus florida* (flowering dogwood)

*Crataegus phaenopyrum*
(Washington hawthorn) (D) (F)
*Picea omorika* (Serbian spruce)
*Pyrus calleryana* 'Bradford'
(Bradford pear) (D) (F)

### Large (more than 40 ft)
*Betula nigra* (river birch) (D)
*Picea abies* (Norway spruce)
*Platanus × acerifolia* (London
plane tree) (D)
*Tilia cordata* 'Glenleven'
(glenleven linden) (D)
*Tsuga canadensis* (Canada hemlock)

### NARROW UPRIGHT

### Small (10-25 ft)
*Acer platanoides* 'Crimson Sentry'
(crimson sentry Norway
maple) (D)
*Juniperus chinensis* 'Columnaris'
(columnar Chinese juniper)
*Malus* 'Sentinel' (sentinel
crabapple) (D) (F)
*Malus tschonoskii* (Tschonoski
crabapple) (D) (F)
*Thuja occidentalis* 'Elegantissima'
(elegantissima arborvitae)

### Medium (25-40 ft)
*Acer rubrum* 'Bowhall'
(Bowhall red maple) (D)
*Carpinus betulus* 'Fastigiata'
(pyramidal European
hornbeam) (D)
*Juniperus virginiana*
(red cedar)
*Malus baccata* 'Columnaris'
(columnar Siberian
crabapple) (D) (F)
*Pyrus calleryana* 'Chanticleer'
(chanticleer callery pear) (D)

### Large (more than 40 ft)
*Acer platanoides* 'Columnare'
(columnar Norway maple) (D)
*Ginkgo biloba* 'Fastigiata'
(fastigiate maidenhair tree) (D)
*Pinus strobus* 'Fastigiata' (fastigiate
eastern white pine)
*Quercus robur* 'Fastigiata'
(fastigiate English oak) (D)

*Tilia americana* 'Fastigiata'
(pyramidal American linden) (D)

## Screens

### Low (5-8 ft)
*Berberis thunbergii*
(Japanese barberry) (D)
*Ilex glabra* 'Compacta'
(Nordic holly)
*Juniperus chinensis* 'Spearmint'
(spearmint juniper)
*Myrica pensylvanica*
(bayberry) (D)
*Taxus × media* 'Chadwickii'
(Chadwicks yew)

### Medium (8-15 ft)
*Ligustrum obtusifolium*
'Regelianum' (Regel privet) (6) (D)
*Rosa rugosa* (rugosa rose) (D) (F)
*Syringa vulgaris* (common
lilac) (D) (F)
*Taxus × media* 'Hicksii' (Hicks yew)
*Viburnum × burkwoodii* (Burkwood
viburnum) (6) (D) (F)

### Tall (more than 15 ft)
*Pinus strobus* 'Fastigiata' (fastigiate
eastern white pine)
*Taxus cuspidata* 'Capitata'
(pyramidal Japanese yew)
*Thuja occidentalis*
(American arborvitae)
*Viburnum lentago*
(nannyberry) (D) (F)

## Informal Hedges
### (less than 5 ft)
*Euonymus alata* (winged euonymus)
*Ilex crenata* (Japanese holly) (6)
*Lonicera xylosteum* 'Claveyii'
(Claveys dwarf honeysuckle)
*Rosa rugosa* (rugosa rose) (D) (F)
*Viburnum dentatum*
(arrowwood) (D) (F)

## Formal Hedges

### Low (less than 3 ft)
*Berberis thunbergii* 'Crimson Pygmy'
(crimson pygmy Japanese
barberry) (D)

*Berberis thunbergii* 'Kobold'
(Kobold Japanese barberry) (D)
*Buxus microphylla*
(littleleaf boxwood) (6)
*Ilex crenata* 'Green Lustre'
(green lustre holly)
*Taxus × media* 'Everlow'
(everlow yew)

### Medium (3-6 ft)
*Berberis koreana* (Korean
barberry) (D)
*Buxus sempervirens* 'Suffruticosa'
(true dwarf boxwood)
*Ilex serrata × I. verticillata*
'Sparkleberry' (sparkleberry,
winterberry)
*Ligustrum obtusifolium*
(border privet) (6)
*Taxus × media* 'Brownii'
(Browns yew)

### Tall (6-15 ft)
*Ilex × meserveae* (blue boy holly,
blue girl holly)
*Ligustrum amurense* (Amur
privet) (D) (F)
*Taxus × media* 'Hicksii' (Hicks yew)
*Tsuga canadensis*
(Canada hemlock)

## Shrubs

### Low (less than 3 ft)
*Berberis thunbergii* 'Crimson Pygmy'
(crimson pygmy barberry) (D)
*Cotoneaster dammeri*
(bearberry cotoneaster)
*Juniperus horizontalis*
(creeping juniper)
*Pinus mugo* var. *mugo* (mugho pine)
*Potentilla fruticosa* (shrubby
cinquefoil) (D) (F)

### Medium (3-6 ft)
*Clethra alnifolia* (summersweet) (F)
*Cotoneaster apiculatus*
(cranberry cotoneaster) (6)
*Juniperus sabina* 'Tamariscifolia'
(Tam juniper)
*Rhododendron* 'P.J.M.' (P.J.M.
rhododendron) (F)
*Syringa meyeri* (Meyer lilac) (D) (F)

*Cotoneaster dammeri* (bearberry cotoneaster)

## Tall (6–15 ft)

*Forsythia × intermedia*
(forsythia) (D) (F)

*Pieris japonica* (Japanese
andromeda) (F)

*Pyracantha* 'Mohave'
(mohave pyracantha)

*Syringa vulgaris* (common
lilac) (D) (F)

*Viburnum plicatum* var.
*tomentosum*
(doublefile viburnum) (F)

## Ground Covers

### Low (less than 4 in.)

*Ajuga reptans* (carpet bugle) (F)

*Galium odorata* (sweet
woodruff) (F)

*Juniperus horizontalis* 'Wiltonii'
(blue rug juniper)

*Thymus praecox arcticus*
(mother-of-thyme)

### Medium (4–12 in.)

*Epimedium* (barrenwort) (D) (F)

*Euonymus fortunei* (wintercreeper)

*Hedera helix* (English ivy)

*Pachysandra terminalis*
(Japanese spurge)

*Vinca minor* (periwinkle) (F)

## Tall (12–30 in.)

Ferns, several species

*Hemerocallis* (daylily, several
varieties) (F)

*Hosta* (plantain lily,
several varieties) (F)

*Juniperus* (juniper, selected
cultivars)

*Paxistima canbyi*
(Canby paxistima)

## Perennials

### Low (less than 10 in.)

*Cerastium tomentosum*
(snow-in-summer) (F)

*Dianthus* (pink) (F)

*Iberis sempervirens* (evergreen
candytuft) (F)

*Liriope muscari* 'Big Blue'
(big blue lilyturf) (F)

*Cerastium tomentosum* (snow-in-summer)

## Medium (10–24 in.)

*Astilbe* (astilbe, several
species) (D) (F)

*Brunnera macrophylla*
(brunnera) (D) (F)

*Lavandula* (lavender) (F)

*Liatris spicata* 'Kobold'
(gayfeather) (D) (F)

## Tall (more than 24 in.)

*Achillea filipendulina*
(fern-leaf yarrow) (F)

*Anemone* × *hybrida*
(Japanese anemone) (D) (F)

*Coreopsis* (coreopsis, several
varieties) (D) (F)

*Echinacea purpurea* (purple
coneflower) (D) (F)

*Hemerocallis* (daylily,
selected cultivars) (D) (F)

# Ornamental Grasses

*Arundo donax* (giant reed)

*Elymus arenarius* (lyme grass)

*Festuca ovina* var. *glauca*
(blue fescue)

*Miscanthus sinensis* 'Zebrinus'
(zebra grass)

*Anemone* × *hybrida* (Japanese anemone)

*Clematis* 'Hagley Hybrid' (pink chiffon clematis)

*Phalaris arundinacea* var. *picta*
(ribbon grass)

# Vines

*Ampelopsis brevipendunculata*
(porcelain vine) (D)

*Aristolochia durior*
(Dutchman's-pipe) (D)

*Campsis radicans*
(trumpet vine) (D) (F)

*Clematis* (clematis, several
species) (D) (F)

*Lonicera japonica* 'Halliana'
(Hall's Japanese
honeysuckle) (D) (F)

*Parthenocissus quinquefolia*
(Virginia creeper) (D)

*Parthenocissus tricuspidata*
(Boston ivy) (D)

*Polygonum aubertii*
(silver lace vine) (D) (F)

*Vitis labrusca* (fox grape) (D)

*Wisteria sinensis*
(Chinese wisteria) (D) (F)

*Miscanthus sinensis* 'Zebrinus' (zebra grass)

## ZONES 7 AND 8

### Shade Trees

#### Small (10-25 ft)

*Acer palmatum* (Japanese
    maple) (D)
*Carpinus caroliniana*
    (American hornbeam) (D)
*Cercis chinensis* (Chinese
    redbud) (D) (F)
*Cornus alternifolia*
    (pagoda dogwood) (D)
*Vitex agnus-castus*
    (chaste tree) (D) (F)

#### Medium (25-40 ft)

*Cercidiphyllum japonicum*
    (katsura tree) (D)
*Oxydendrum arboreum*
    (sourwood) (D) (F)
*Sapium sebiferum*
    (Chinese tallow tree) (D)
*Ulmus alata* (winged elm) (D)
*Ulmus parvifolia* (Chinese elm,
    lacebark elm) (D)

#### Large (more than 40 ft)

*Acer rubrum* (red maple) (D)
*Acer saccharinum* (silver maple) (D)
*Carya illinoinensis* (pecan) (D)
*Fagus grandifolia*
    (American beech) (D)
*Ginkgo biloba*
    (maidenhair tree) (D)
*Quercus phellos* (willow oak) (D)

## Landscape Trees

### BROAD SPREADING

#### Small (10-25 ft)

*Arbutus unedo* (strawberry
    tree) (8) (F)
*Eriobotrya japonica* (loquat) (8)
*Ilex cornuta* 'Burfordii'
    (Burford Chinese holly)
*Pinus thunbergiana*
    (Japanese black pine)
*Prunus caroliniana* (cherry laurel)

#### Medium (25-40 ft)

*Ilex opaca* (American holly)

*Lagerstroemia indica* (crape myrtle)

*Ligustrum lucidum*
    (glossy privet) (F)
*Magnolia virginiana*
    (sweet bay magnolia) (F)
*Pinus glabra* (spruce pine) (8)
*Quercus acuta* (Japanese
    evergreen oak)

#### Large (more than 40 ft)

*Cupressus arizonica*
    (Arizona cypress)
*Magnolia grandiflora*
    (southern magnolia) (F)
*Pinus strobus* (eastern white pine)

*Quercus laurifolia* (laurel oak)
*Quercus virginiana* (live oak)

### OVAL UPRIGHT TO PYRAMIDAL

#### Small (10-25 ft)

*Ilex aquifolium* × *I. cornuta* 'Nellie
    R. Stevens' (Nellie Stevens holly)
*Ilex cassine* (cassine holly, dahoon)
*Ilex vomitoria* (yaupon holly)
*Lagerstroemia indica*
    (crape myrtle) (D) (F)
*Laurus nobilis* (sweet bay,
    Grecian laurel)

### Medium (25-40 ft)

*Crataegus opaca* (may haw) (D) (F)
*Crataegus phaenopyrum*
　(Washington hawthorn) (D) (F)
*Diospyros virginiana*
　(common persimmon) (D)
*Ilex × attenuata* 'Foster No. 2'
　(Foster no. 2 holly)
*Magnolia heptapeta*
　(Yulan magnolia) (D) (F)

### Large (more than 40 ft)

*Cedrus atlantica* (atlas cedar)
*Cedrus deodara* (deodar cedar)
*Cunninghamia lanceolata*
　(China fir)
*Juniperus virginiana* (red cedar)
*Liquidambar styraciflua*
　(sweet gum) (D)

### NARROW UPRIGHT

### Small (10-25 ft)

*Hibiscus syriacus*
　(shrub althaea) (D) (F)
*Ilex latifolia* (lusterleaf holly)
*Juniperus chinensis* 'Columnaris'
　(Chinese blue column juniper)
*Malus* 'Van Eseltine'
　(Van Eseltine crabapple) (D) (F)
*Prunus serrulata* 'Amanogawa'
　(Japanese flowering
　cherry) (D) (F)

### Medium (25-40 ft)

*Aralia spinosa* (devils walking
　stick) (D)
*Carpinus betulus* 'Columnaris'
　(columnar European
　hornbeam) (D)
*Cleyera japonica* (Japanese cleyera)
*Podocarpus macrophyllus*
　(yew pine) (8)
*Taxus baccata* 'Stricta' (Irish yew)

### Large (more than 40 ft)

× *Cupressocyparis leylandii* 'Green
　Spire' (green spire cypress)
× *Cupressocyparis leylandii*
　'Naylors Blue' (Naylors
　blue cypress)
*Cupressus sempervirens* 'Stricta'
　(Italian cypress)

*Populus nigra* 'Italica'
　(Lombardy poplar) (D)
*Populus tremula* 'Erecta' (upright
　European aspen) (D)

## Screens

### Low (5-8 ft)

*Berberis thunbergii* (Japanese
　barberry) (D)
*Ilex cornuta* 'Burfordii Nana'
　(dwarf Burford holly)
*Ligustrum lucidum*
　(glossy privet ) (F)
*Photinia glabra* (Japanese photinia)
*Raphiolepis indica*
　(India-hawthorn) (F)

### Medium (8-15 ft)

*Elaeagnus pungens* 'Fruitlandii'
　(fruitland elaeagnus)
*Ilex cornuta* 'Burfordii'
　(Burford holly)
*Osmanthus × fortunei*
　(Fortunes osmanthus)
*Photinia × 'Fraseri'
　(redtip, Fraser photinia)
*Prunus laurocerasus*
　(English laurel)

### Tall (more than 15 ft)

*Cinnamomum camphora*
　(camphor tree) (8)
× *Cupressocyparis leylandii*
　(Leyland cypress)
*Pinus strobus* (eastern
　white pine) (7)
*Pinus virginiana* (Virginia pine)
*Tsuga canadensis*
　(Canada hemlock) (7)

## Informal Hedges
### (less than 5 ft)

*Abelia × grandiflora* 'Sherwoodii'
　(Sherwood dwarf abelia) (F)
*Berberis thunbergii* 'Atropurpurea'
　(red Japanese barberry) (D)
*Chaenomeles japonica* (Japanese
　flowering quince) (D) (F)
*Cotoneaster horizontalis*
　(rock cotoneaster)
*Rosa* of the Floribunda class
　(floribunda rose hybrids) (D) (F)

## Formal Hedges

### Low (less than 3 ft)

*Berberis thunbergii* 'Crimson
　Pygmy' (crimson pygmy Japanese
　barberry) (D)
*Buxus microphylla* var. *koreana*
　(Korean boxwood)
*Ilex crenata* 'Repandens'
　(repandens holly)
*Nandina domestica* 'Harbour Dwarf'
　(harbour dwarf nandina)
*Teucrium chamaedrys*
　(germander) (F)

### Medium (3-6 ft)

*Buxus microphylla* var. *japonica*
　(Japanese boxwood)
*Buxus sempervirens*
　(common boxwood)
*Juniperus chinensis* 'Armstrongii'
　(Armstrong juniper)
*Spiraea cantoniensis* (bridal
　wreath spirea) (D) (F)
*Spiraea thunbergii*
　(Thunberg spirea) (D) (F)

### Tall (6-15 ft)

× *Cupressocyparis leylandii*
　(Leyland cypress)
*Ilex cassine* (cassine holly)
*Ilex vomitoria* (yaupon holly)
*Pinus strobus* (eastern
　white pine) (7)
*Tsuga canadensis*
　(Canada hemlock) (7)

## Shrubs

### Low (less than 3 ft)

*Aucuba japonica* 'Nana'
　(Japanese dwarf aucuba)
*Daphne odora* (winter daphne) (F)
*Gardenia* 'Radicans'
　(creeping gardenia) (F)
*Ilex crenata* 'Helleri' (Heller
　Japanese holly)
*Ilex crenata* 'Repandens'
　(repandens holly)

### Medium (3-6 ft)

*Ilex cornuta* 'Carissa' (carissa holly)

*Viburnum davidii* (David viburnum)

*Ilex vomitoria* 'Nana'
(dwarf yaupon holly)
*Jasminum floridum*
(showy jasmine) (F)
*Leucothoe axillaris*
(coastal leucothoe) (F)

## Tall (6–15 ft)
*Aucuba japonica* (Japanese aucuba)
*Forsythia* × *intermedia*
(forsythia) (D) (F)
*Hydrangea paniculata* 'Grandiflora'
(peegee hydrangea) (D) (F)
*Ilex cornuta* 'Burfordii'
(Burford holly)
*Osmanthus heterophyllus* 'Gulftide'
(gulftide tea olive)

## Ground Covers

### Low (less than 4 in.)
*Ajuga reptans* (carpet bugle) (F)
*Juniperus horizontalis* 'Wiltonii'
(blue rug juniper)
*Phlox subulata* (moss pink) (F)
*Sedum acre* (yellow
stonecrop) (F)
*Thymus praecox arcticus*
(mother-of-thyme) (F)

*Daphne odora* 'Marginata' (winter daphne)

### Medium (4–12 in.)

*Hypericum calycinum* (Aarons-
   beard, St. Johnswort) (F)
*Juniperus conferta* 'Blue Pacific'
   (blue Pacific juniper)
*Liriope muscari* (lilyturf) (F)
*Ophiopogon japonicus*
   (mondo grass)
*Santolina chamaecyparissus*
   (lavender cotton) (F)

### Tall (12–30 in.)

*Gardenia* 'Radicans'
   (creeping gardenia) (F)
*Hemerocallis fulva* (daylily) (D) (F)
*Juniperus chinensis* 'Parsonii'
   (Parsons juniper)
*Juniperus chinensis* 'Sargentii'
   (Sargent juniper)
*Rosmarinus officinalis* 'Prostratus'
   (prostrate rosemary) (F)

## Perennials

### Low (less than 10 in.)

*Hyacinthus orientalis*
   (Dutch hyacinth) (D) (F)
*Iberis sempervirens*
   (evergreen candytuft) (F)
*Oxalis rubra* (wood sorrel) (D) (F)
*Saxifraga stolonifera*
   (strawberry geranium) (F)
*Trillium* (trillium) (D) (F)
*Viola odorata* (sweet violet) (D) (F)

### Medium (10–24 in.)

*Chrysanthemum* × *superbum*
   (Shasta daisy) (D) (F)
*Dianthus deltoides* (maiden
   pink) (F)
*Hosta* (plantain lily) (D) (F)
*Iris xiphium* (Dutch iris) (D) (F)
*Leucojum vernum*
   (snowdrop) (D) (F)

### Tall (more than 24 in.)

*Canna* × *generalis*
   (canna) (D) (F)
*Helianthus* (wild
   sunflower) (D) (F)

*Mirabilis jalapa*
   (four-o'clock) (D) (F)
*Phlox paniculata*
   (summer phlox) (D) (F)
*Rudbeckia maxima*
   (coneflower) (D) (F)

## Ornamental Grasses

*Cortaderia selloana* (pampas grass)
*Festuca ovina* var. *glauca*
   (blue fescue)
*Miscanthus sinensis* 'Zebrinus'
   (zebra grass) (D)
*Pennisetum setaceum*
   (fountain grass) (D)
*Stipa pennata* (European
   feather grass)

## Vines

*Akebia quinata* (five-leaf akebia)
*Ampelopsis brevipedunculata*
   (porcelain vine) (D)
*Campsis radicans* (trumpet
   vine) (D) (F)
*Clematis dioscoreifolia*
   (sweet autumn clematis) (D) (F)
*Gelsemium sempervirens*
   (Carolina jessamine) (F)
*Hedera helix* (English ivy)
*Lonicera sempervirens*
   (coral honeysuckle) (F)
*Parthenocissus quinquefolia*
   (Virginia creeper) (D)
*Smilax lanceolata* (smilax)
*Wisteria sinensis* (Chinese
   wisteria) (D) (F)

*Helianthus angustifolius* (sunflower)

*Phlox paniculata alba* (white summer phlox)

## ZONES 9 AND 10

### Shade Trees

#### Small (10–25 ft)

*Acer palmatum* (Japanese maple) (D)
*Cercis canadensis* (redbud) (D) (F)
*Lagerstroemia indica* (crape myrtle) (D) (F)
*Malus* (flowering crabapple cultivars) (D) (F)
*Vitex agnus-castus* (chaste tree) (D) (F)

#### Medium (25–40 ft)

*Albizia julibrissin* (silk tree, mimosa) (D) (F)
*Fraxinus oxycarpa* 'Raywood' (Raywood ash) (D)
*Koelreuteria paniculata* (goldenrain tree) (D) (F)
*Sapium sebiferum* (Chinese tallow tree) (D)
*Sophora japonica* (Japanese pagoda tree) (D) (F)
*Styrax japonicus* (Japanese snowdrop tree) (D) (F)

#### Large (more than 40 ft)

*Acer saccharinum* (silver maple) (D)
*Liriodendron tulipifera* (tulip tree) (D) (F)
*Nyssa sylvatica* (black gum, tupelo) (D)
*Paulownia tomentosa* (empress tree) (D) (F)
*Pistacia chinensis* (Chinese pistache) (D)
*Tipuana tipu* (tipu tree) (D) (F)

### Landscape Trees

#### BROAD SPREADING

#### Small (10–25 ft)

*Eriobotrya deflexa* (bronze loquat)
*Magnolia grandiflora* 'St. Mary' (St. Mary magnolia) (F)
*Olea europaea* (olive)
*Pittosporum undulatum* (Victorian box)
*Rhus lancea* (African sumac)

*Acacia baileyana* (Bailey acacia)

#### Medium (25–40 ft)

*Acacia baileyana* (Bailey acacia) (F)
*Agonis flexuosa* (peppermint tree) (10)
*Ligustrum lucidum* (glossy privet) (F)
*Maytenus boaria* (mayten tree)
*Podocarpus gracilior* (fern pine)

#### Large (more than 40 ft)

*Calodendrum capense* (cape chestnut) (10)
*Cinnamomum camphora* (camphor tree)
*Magnolia grandiflora* (southern magnolia) (F)
*Pinus pinea* (Italian stone pine)
*Quercus suber* (cork oak)

## OVAL UPRIGHT TO PYRAMIDAL

### Small (10–25 ft)
*Ficus retusa* (Indian laurel)
*Hymenosporum flavum* (sweetshade) (F)
*Lagerstroemia indica* (crape myrtle) (D) (F)
*Laurus nobilis* (sweet bay, Grecian laurel)
*Prunus cerasifera* 'Krauter Vesuvius' (purpleleaf plum) (D) (F)

### Medium (25–40 ft)
*Eucalyptus nicholii* (Nichol's willow-leafed peppermint) (F)
*Lagunaria patersonii* (primrose tree) (F)
*Pittosporum undulatum* (Victorian box)
*Pyrus calleryana* 'Bradford' (Bradford pear) (D) (F)
*Stenocarpus sinuatus* (firewheel tree) (10) (F)

### Large (more than 40 ft)
*Eucalyptus viminalis* (manna gum)
*Fagus grandifolia* (American beech) (D)
*Pinus canariensis* (Canary Island pine)
*Quercus palustris* (pin oak) (D)
*Taxodium distichum* (bald cypress) (D)

## NARROW UPRIGHT

### Small (10–25 ft)
*Crataegus × lavallei* (Carriere hawthorn) (D) (F)
*Juniperus chinensis* 'Columnaris' (Chinese blue column juniper)
*Juniperus communis* 'Stricta' (Irish juniper)
*Malus baccata* 'Columnaris' (columnar Siberian crabapple) (D) (F)
*Podocarpus macrophyllus* 'Maki' (shrubby yew pine)

### Medium (25–40 ft)
*Malus tschonoskii* (Tschonoski crabapple) (D) (F)
*Melaleuca quinquenervia* (cajeput tree) (F)
*Quercus robur* 'Fastigiata' (fastigiate English oak) (D)
*Taxus baccata* 'Stricta' (Irish yew)
*Trachycarpus fortunei* (windmill palm)

### Large (more than 40 ft)
*Cupressus sempervirens* 'Stricta' (Italian cypress)
*Liriodendron tulipifera* 'Arnold' (Arnold tulip tree) (D) (F)
*Populus nigra* 'Italica' (Lombardy poplar) (D)
*Robinia pseudoacacia* 'Pyramidalis' (fastigiate black locust) (D) (F)
*Washingtonia robusta* (Mexican fan palm)

## Screens

### Low (5–8 ft)
*Abelia × grandiflora* (glossy abelia) (F)
*Choisya ternata* (Mexican orange) (F)
*Myrtus communis* 'Compacta' (dwarf myrtle) (F)
*Ternstroemia gymnanthera* (Japan cleyera, ternstroemia)

*Viburnum tinus* 'Spring Bouquet' (spring bouquet laurustinus) (F)

### Medium (8–15 ft)
*Arbutus unedo* (strawberry tree) (F)
*Elaeagnus pungens* (silverberry)
*Jasminum mesnyi* (primrose jasmine) (F)
*Photinia × fraseri* (Fraser photinia)
*Rhus integrifolia* (lemonade berry)

### Tall (more than 15 ft)
*Feijoa sellowiana* (pineapple guava) (F)
*Griselinia littoralis* (griselinia)
*Osmanthus fragrans* (fragrant sweet olive)
*Pittosporum eugenioides* (tarata)
*Prunus lusitanica* (Portugal laurel) (F)

## Informal Hedges
### (less than 5 ft)
*Juniperus chinensis* 'Armstrongii' (Armstrong juniper)
*Lavandula* (all species of lavender) (F)
*Rosa* of the Floribunda class (floribunda rose hybrids) (D) (F)
*Rosmarinus officinalis* 'Tuscan Blue' (Tuscan blue rosemary) (F)
*Sarcococca ruscifolia* (sarcococca)

*Choisya ternata* (Mexican orange)

## Formal Hedges

### Low (less than 3 ft)

*Buxus microphylla japonica*
  (Japanese boxwood)
*Hebe buxifolia* (boxleaf hebe) (F)
*Ilex vomitoria* 'Nana'
  (dwarf yaupon)
*Punica granatum* 'Nana'
  (dwarf pomegranate) (D) (F)
*Teucrium chamaedrys*
  (germander) (F)

### Medium (3–6 ft)

*Abelia* × *grandiflora*
  (glossy abelia) (F)
*Escallonia* × *exoniensis* 'Frades'
  (Frades escallonia) (F)
*Leptospermum scoparium* 'Ruby
  Glow' (ruby glow New Zealand
  tea tree) (F)
*Myrsine africana* (African boxwood)
*Myrtus communis* (myrtle) (F)

### Tall (6–15 ft)

*Pittosporum tenuifolium* (tawhiwhi)
*Podocarpus macrophyllus*
  (yew pine)
*Rhamnus alaternus* (Italian
  buckthorn)
*Syzygium paniculatum* (Australian
  brush cherry)
*Xylosma congestum* (shiny xylosma)

## Shrubs

### Low (less than 3 ft)

*Escallonia* 'Newport Dwarf'
  (Newport dwarf escallonia) (F)
*Lantana montevidensis* (trailing
  lantana) (F)
*Pittosporum tobira* 'Wheeleri'
  (Wheelers dwarf tobira)
*Raphiolepis indica* 'Ballerina'
  (ballerina India-hawthorn) (F)
*Viburnum davidii*
  (David viburnum) (F)

### Medium (3–6 ft)

*Daphne odora* (winter daphne) (F)
*Gardenia jasminoides* (Cape
  jasmine, gardenia) (F)

*Raphiolepis indica* (India-hawthorn)

*Nerium oleander* (oleander)

*Pittosporum tobira* 'Variegata'
  (variegated tobira)
*Plumbago auriculata*
  (Cape leadwort) (F)
*Viburnum suspensum* (sandankwa
  viburnum) (F)

### Tall (6–15 ft)

*Camellia japonica* (common
  camellia) (F)
*Cotoneaster lacteus*
  (red clusterberry)
*Hibiscus rosa-sinensis* (Chinese
  hibiscus) (10) (F)
*Michelia figo* (banana-shrub) (F)
*Nerium oleander* (oleander) (F)

## Ground Covers

### Low (less than 4 in.)

*Fragaria chiloensis* (ornamental
  strawberry) (F)
*Laurentia fluviatilis* (bluestar
  creeper) (F)
*Soleirolia soleirolii* (babytears)
*Thymus praecox arcticus*
  (mother-of-thyme) (F)

### Medium (4–12 in.)

*Carissa grandiflora* 'Green Carpet'
  (green carpet natal plum) (F)
*Gazania rigens* var. *leucolaena*
  (trailing gazania) (F)

*Ophiopogon japonicus* (mondo grass)
*Pelargonium peltatum* (ivy
     geranium) (F)
*Stachys byzantina* (woolly
     lambs ears) (F)

## Tall (12–30 in.)

*Baccharis pilularis* (dwarf
     coyote brush)
*Cotoneaster dammeri* 'Coral Beauty'
     (coral beauty bearberry
     cotoneaster)
*Rosmarinus officinalis* 'Prostratus'
     (prostrate rosemary) (F)
*Sollya heterophylla* (Australian
     bluebell creeper) (F)
*Trachelospermum jasminoides*
     (star jasmine) (F)

## Perennials

### Low (less than 10 in.)

*Aurinia saxatilis*
     (basket-of-gold) (F)
*Bergenia crassifolia* (winter-
     blooming bergenia) (F)
*Geranium* (cranesbill) (F)

*Heuchera micrantha*
     (coral bells) (F)
*Iberis sempervirens* (evergreen
     candytuft) (F)

### Medium (10–24 in.)

*Agapanthus africanus* 'Peter Pan'
     (Peter Pan agapanthus) (F)
*Limonium perezii* (sea lavender) (F)
*Penstemon gloxinioides*
     (beard tongue) (F)
*Scabiosa columbaria* (pincushion
     flower) (F)

### Tall (more than 24 in.)

*Aconitum napellus*
     (monkshood) (D) (F)
*Delphinium elatum*
     (delphinium, selected
     cultivars) (D) (F)
*Salvia leucantha* (Mexican
     bush sage) (F)
*Verbena bonariensis*
     (vervain) (D) (F)
*Watsonia pyramidata*
     (watsonia, selected
     cultivars) (D) (F)

## Ornamental Grasses

*Cyperus papyrus* (papyrus)
*Deschampsia caespitosa*
     (tufted hair grass)
*Festuca ovina* var. *glauca*
     (blue fescue)
*Helictotrichon sempervirens*
     (blue oat grass)
*Stipa gigantea* (giant feather grass)

## Vines

*Actinidia chinensis* (kiwi berry) (D)
*Bougainvillea spectabilis*
     (bougainvillea) (10) (F)
*Clematis armandii* (evergreen
     clematis) (F)
*Clytostoma callistegioides* (lavender
     trumpet vine) (F)
*Ficus pumila* (creeping fig)
*Gelsemium sempervirens* (Carolina
     jessamine) (F)
*Jasminum polyanthum*
     (pink jasmine) (F)
*Parthenocissus tricuspidata*
     (Boston ivy) (D)
*Rhoicissus capensis*
     (evergreen grape)

*Festuca ovina* var. *glauca* (blue fescue)

*Clytostoma callistegioides* (lavender trumpet vine)

## Landscape Designers and Architects and Site Credits

The landscape plans in this book represent as-built designs and are based on site research, and on information provided by homeowners and the designers; changes have often occurred from the original design intent. Many of the gardens were designed and/or executed in collaboration with the owners.

Front cover: Ransohoff, Blanchfield, Jones, Redwood City, Calif. (garden design); Robert Morrell and CSM Master Pools, Belmont, Calif. (pool design)

Page 4: Designer uncertain

Page 7: Jonathan Plant Associates, Lafayette, Calif.

Page 8: Thomas D. Church (orignal garden design); remodeled by Bassett & Ciofalo, San Francisco, Calif.

Page 10: Designer unknown

Page 11: Kathryn Mathewson Associates, San Francisco, Calif.

Page 12T: Thomas D. Church (original garden design); remodeled by Bassett & Ciofalo, San Francisco, Calif.

Page 12B: Ron Lutsko, Jr. & Associates, San Francisco, Calif.

Page13T: Thomas D. Church

Page 13B: Meecham-O'Brien, San Francisco, Calif.

Page 14T: Designer unknown, Kings Park, N.Y.

Page 14B: T. Delaney Construction, San Rafael, Calif.

Page 15: Thomas D. Church

Page 16T: Designer unknown, Long Island, N.Y.

Page 16B: T. Delaney Construction, San Rafael, Calif.

Page 17: Ransohoff, Blanchfield, Jones, Redwood City, Calif.

Page 20: Thomas D. Church

Pages 22–23: Jonathan Plant Associates, Lafayette, Calif.

Pages 24–25: Gertrud Aronstein (original garden design); remodeled by Thomas D. Church

Pages 26–27: Henning Associates, Oakland, Calif.

Pages 28–29: Deck plantings designed by owner, Stinson Beach, Calif.; ceramic sculpture by Peter Voulkos

Pages 30–31: Ransohoff, Blanchfield, Jones, Redwood City, Calif.

Pages 32–33: Kathryn Mathewson Associates, San Francisco, Calif.

Pages 34–35: Kathryn Mathewson Associates, San Francisco, Calif.

Pages 36–37: Designer unknown

Pages 38–39: Babcock-Hansen, Lafayette, Calif.

Pages 40–41: Henry Cole, San Rafael, Calif.

Page 42: Barbara Chevalier, A.S.I.D., Barbara Chevalier Interiors, San Francisco, Calif. (garden design), original designer unknown; Valentino Agnoli, Stinson Beach, Calif. (pool design)

Page 43: Thomas D. Church (garden design); pool designer unknown

Pages 44–45: Collver Water Garden design and plantings by owners, Mitsuko and Andrew Collver, Stony Brook, N.Y.

Pages 46–47: Kathryn Mathewson Associates, San Francisco, Calif.

Page 48: Blake Gardens, Kensington, Calif.

Page 49: Designer unknown, Portland, Ore.

Pages 50–51: Jonathan Plant Associates, Lafayette, Calif.

Pages 52–53: Ron Lutsko, Jr. & Associates, San Francisco, Calif.

Pages 54–55: Designer unknown

Pages 56–57: Barbara Chevalier, A.S.I.D., Barbara Chevalier Interiors, San Francisco, Calif. (garden design), original designer unknown

Page 58: Ransohoff, Blanchfield, Jones, Redwood City, Calif.

Page 59: Designer unknown

Page 60: Designer unknown

Page 61T: Filoli Gardens, Woodside, Calif.

Page 61B: Designer unknown, Harbor Heights, N.Y.

Pages 62–63: Green & Tyson Landscaping, San Anselmo, Calif.

Pages 64–65: Ron Lutsko, Jr. & Associates, San Francisco, Calif.

Pages 66–67: Jonathan Plant Associates, Lafayette, Calif. (plant selection and path design)

Pages 68–69: Ron Lutsko, Jr. & Associates, San Francisco, Calif.

Pages 70–71: Marion Panaretos, Hillsborough, Calif.

Pages 72–73: Designer unknown, Lloyd Neck, N.Y.

Pages 74–75: Thomas D. Church

Pages 76–77: Ron Lutsko, Jr. & Associates, San Francisco, Calif.

Pages 78–79: Jonathan Plant Associates, Lafayette, Calif. (planting design); David Arbegast, Berkeley, Calif. (patio design)

Pages 80–81: Ron Lutsko, Jr. & Associates, San Francisco, Calif.

Pages 82–83: Meecham-O'Brien, San Francisco, Calif.

Pages 84–85: Henning Associates, Oakland, Calif.

Page 86: Barbara Chevalier, A.S.I.D., Barbara Chevalier Interiors, San Francisco, Calif. (garden design), original designer unknown

## U.S. Measure and Metric Measure Conversion Chart

| | | Formulas for Exact Measures | | | Rounded Measures for Quick Reference | | |
|---|---|---|---|---|---|---|---|
| | Symbol | When you know: | Multiply by: | To find: | | | |
| **Mass (Weight)** | oz | ounces | 28.35 | grams | 1 oz | | = 30 g |
| | lb | pounds | 0.45 | kilograms | 4 oz | | = 115 g |
| | g | grams | 0.035 | ounces | 8 oz | | = 225 g |
| | kg | kilograms | 2.2 | pounds | 16 oz | = 1 lb | = 450 g |
| | | | | | 32 oz | = 2 lb | = 900 g |
| | | | | | 36 oz | = 2¼ lb | = 1000g (1 kg) |
| **Volume** | pt | pints | 0.47 | liters | 1 c | = 8 oz | = 250 ml |
| | qt | quarts | 0.95 | liters | 2 c (1 pt) | = 16 oz | = 500 ml |
| | gal | gallons | 3.785 | liters | 4 c (1 qt) | = 32 oz | = 1 liter |
| | ml | milliliters | 0.034 | fluid ounces | 4 qt (1 gal) | = 128 oz | = 3¾ liter |
| **Length** | in. | inches | 2.54 | centimeters | ⅜ in. | | = 1 cm |
| | ft | feet | 30.48 | centimeters | 1 in. | | = 2.5 cm |
| | yd | yards | 0.9144 | meters | 2 in. | | = 5 cm |
| | mi | miles | 1.609 | kilometers | 2½ in. | | = 6.5 cm |
| | km | kilometers | 0.621 | miles | 12 in. (1 ft) | | = 30 cm |
| | m | meters | 1.094 | yards | 1 yd | | = 90 cm |
| | cm | centimeters | 0.39 | inches | 100 ft | | = 30 m |
| | | | | | 1 mi | | = 1.6 km |
| **Temperature** | °F | Fahrenheit | ⅚ (after subtracting 32) | Celsius | 32°F | | = 0°C |
| | °C | Celsius | ⅚ (then add 32) | Fahrenheit | 212°F | | = 100°C |
| **Area** | in.² | square inches | 6.452 | square centimeters | 1 in.² | | = 6.5 cm² |
| | ft² | square feet | 929.0 | square centimeters | 1 ft² | | = 930 cm² |
| | yd² | square yards | 8361.0 | square centimeters | 1 yd² | | = 8360 cm² |
| | a. | acres | 0.4047 | hectares | 1 a. | | = 4050 m² |